PRISM

READING AND WRITING

2

Carolyn Westbrook
Lida Baker

with
Wendy Asplin
Janet Gokay

CAMBRIDGE
UNIVERSITY PRESS

CAMBRIDGE
UNIVERSITY PRESS

University Printing House, Cambridge CB2 8BS, United Kingdom

One Liberty Plaza, 20th Floor, New York, NY 10006, USA

477 Williamstown Road, Port Melbourne, VIC 3207, Australia

4843/24, 2nd Floor, Ansari Road, Daryaganj, Delhi – 110002, India

79 Anson Road, #06–04/06, Singapore 079906

Cambridge University Press is part of the University of Cambridge.

It furthers the University's mission by disseminating knowledge in the pursuit of education, learning and research at the highest international levels of excellence.

www.cambridge.org
Information on this title: www.cambridge.org/9781316624319

First published 2017
20 19 18 17 16 15 14 13 12 11 10 9 8 7 6 5 4 3 2 1

Printed in Dubai by Oriental Press

A catalogue record for this publication is available from the British Library

ISBN 978-1-316-62431-9 Student's Book with Online Workbook 2 Reading and Writing
ISBN 978-1-316-62513-2 Teacher's Manual 2 Reading and Writing

CONTENTS

SCOPE AND SEQUENCE

UNIT	WATCH AND LISTEN	READINGS	READING SKILLS	LANGUAGE DEVELOPMENT	
1 ANIMALS *Academic Disciplines* Ecology / Zoology	Great Egret and Dolphin Fishing Teamwork	1: Endangered species (factsheet) 2: Losing the Battle for Survival (article)	*Key Skill* Reading for main ideas *Additional Skills* Understanding key vocabulary Using your knowledge Reading for details Working out meaning Summarizing Making inferences Synthesizing	Academic verbs Comparative adjectives	
2 THE ENVIRONMENT *Academic Disciplines* Environmental Science / Natural Science	Colorado River, Grand Canyon, Yosemite	1: Our Changing Planet (web page) 2: The Causes and Effects of Deforestation (essay)	*Key Skill* Reading for details *Additional Skills* Understanding key vocabulary Predicting content using visuals Reading for main ideas Scanning to find information Identifying purpose Previewing Summarizing Making inferences Synthesizing	Academic vocabulary Environment collocations	
3 TRANSPORTATION *Academic Disciplines* Transportation Management / Urban Planning	The Jumbo Jet	1: Masdar: the Future of Cities? (case study) 2: A reading about traffic congestion (essay)	*Key Skill* Predicting content using visuals *Additional Skills* Understanding key vocabulary Reading for main ideas Reading for details Making inferences Synthesizing	Transportation collocations Synonyms for verbs	
4 CUSTOMS AND TRADITIONS *Academic Disciplines* Cultural Studies / Sociology	Halloween by the Numbers	1: Customs Around the World (article) 2: Nontraditional Weddings (article)	*Key Skill* Annotating *Additional Skills* Understanding key vocabulary Using your knowledge Reading for main ideas Reading for details Making inferences Previewing Synthesizing	Avoiding generalizations Adverbs of frequency Synonyms to avoid repetition	

CRITICAL THINKING	GRAMMAR FOR WRITING	WRITING	ON CAMPUS
Use a Venn diagram	Word order Combining sentences • *and* and *or* • *but* and *whereas* • *both* and *neither*	*Academic Writing Skills* Topic sentences *Rhetorical Mode* Comparison and contrast *Writing Task* Compare and contrast the two sharks in the diagram. (essay completion)	*Research Skill* Avoiding plagiarism
Use a cause-effect chart	Verbs of cause and effect *Because* and *because of*	*Academic Writing Skills* Paragraph unity Supporting sentences and details *Rhetorical Mode* Cause and effect *Writing Task* Describe the human causes of climate change and the effects that climate change will have on the planet. (essay completion)	*Life Skill* Choosing your courses
Identify and evaluate problems and solutions	Future real conditional *if … not* and *unless*	*Academic Writing Skill* Writing a concluding sentence *Rhetorical Mode* Problem and solution *Writing Task* Discuss the advantages and disadvantages of two solutions to a city's traffic congestion problems. (essay completion)	*Study Skill* Creating idea maps
Analyze a text Evaluate and respond to an author's ideas	Paraphrasing	*Academic Writing Skills* Writing a summary and a personal response *Rhetorical Mode* Summary and response *Writing Task* Summarize and respond to Reading 2. Give your opinions about the changes in wedding traditions. (paragraphs)	*Communications Skills* Communicating with professors

UNIT	WATCH AND LISTEN	READINGS	READING SKILLS	LANGUAGE DEVELOPMENT	
5 HEALTH AND FITNESS *Academic Disciplines* Medicine / Nutrition	Nutrition Labels	1: A reading about health and exercise (article) 2: Tackling Obesity (essay)	*Key Skill* Making inferences *Additional Skills* Understanding key vocabulary Predicting content using visuals Skimming Reading for main ideas Reading for details Using your knowledge Scanning to predict content Synthesizing	Verb and noun forms Health and fitness collocations	
6 DISCOVERY AND INVENTION *Academic Disciplines* Industrial Design / Mechanical Engineering	China's Man-made River	1: The Magic of Mimicry (article) 2: The World of Tomorrow (article)	*Key Skill* Scanning to find information *Additional Skills* Understanding key vocabulary Using your knowledge Reading for main ideas Annotating Making inferences Reading for details Synthesizing	Making predictions with modals and adverbs of certainty Prefixes	
7 FASHION *Academic Disciplines* Fashion Design / Retail Management	A Life Tailored Around Clothes	1: Is Fast Fashion Taking Over? (article) 2: Offshore Production (essay)	*Key Skills* Distinguishing fact from opinion *Additional Skills* Understanding key vocabulary Using your knowledge Reading for main ideas Reading for details Making inferences Skimming Scanning to find information Synthesizing	Vocabulary for the fashion business	
8 ECONOMICS *Academic Disciplines* Business / Economics	The Stock Market Crash of 1929	1: How Should You Invest Your Money? (article) 2: Income and Expenditure, 1996-2014 (article)	*Key Skills* Skimming *Additional Skills* Understanding key vocabulary Using your knowledge Reading for main ideas Reading for details Making inferences Annotating Synthesizing	Nouns and adjectives for economics Nouns for economic trends	

CRITICAL THINKING	GRAMMAR FOR WRITING	WRITING	ON CAMPUS
Subdivide arguments	Stating opinions Stating a purpose	*Academic Writing Skills* Essay structure *Rhetorical Mode* Opinion *Writing Task* Should colleges and universities require students to take physical education classes? (essay)	*Study Skill* Avoiding procrastination
Use T-charts to brainstorm and organize ideas	Relative clauses Prepositional phrases with advantages and disadvantages	*Academic Writing Skill* Writing an introductory paragraph *Rhetorical Mode* Explanatory *Writing Task* Choose a new area of technology or invention and discuss its advantages and disadvantages. (essay)	*Study Skill* Annotating texts
Identify and strengthen arguments	Multiword prepositions	*Academic Writing Skills* Body paragraphs in argumentative essays Cohesion *Rhetorical Mode* Argumentative *Writing Task* The fashion industry is harmful to society and the environment. Do you agree or disagree? (essay)	*Research Skill* Using Internet sources
Understand and interpret line graphs	Describing graphs—noun phrases and verb phrases Prepositions and conjunctions Approximations	*Academic Writing Skill* Writing a concluding paragraph *Rhetorical Mode* Analysis *Writing Task* Describe the multiple-line graph showing home video revenue and explain the data. (essay)	*Life Skill* College applications

HOW *PRISM* WORKS

1 Video

Setting the context

Every unit begins with a video clip. Each video serves as a springboard for the unit and introduces the topic in an engaging way. The clips were carefully selected to pique students' interest and prepare them to explore the unit's topic in greater depth. As they work, students develop key skills in prediction, comprehension, and discussion.

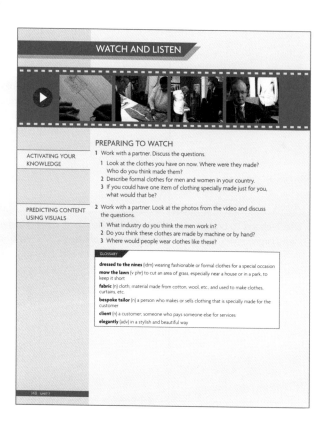

2 Reading

Receptive, language, and analytical skills

Students improve their reading abilities through a sequence of proven activities. They study key vocabulary to prepare them for each reading and to develop academic reading skills. A second reading leads into synthesis exercises that prepare students for college classrooms. Language Development sections teach vocabulary, collocations, and language structure.

READING

READING 1

PREPARING TO READ

Predicting content using visuals

The images that accompany a text can provide valuable information about the content. For example, they can tell you where the text is set, what it is about, what kind of text it is (essay, blog post, etc.), what the key points are, and much more. All this information helps you make predictions about what you are going to read, and once you start reading, it helps you focus on the important information in the reading.

PREDICTING CONTENT USING VISUALS

1 Work with a partner. You are going to read a case study about a new kind of city. Before you read, look at the photos of transportation in two cities and answer the questions.

1 What problem can you see in the first photo? Does your city have this problem?

2 What is the vehicle in the second photo? How could it be a solution to the problem in Question 1? Where do you think the photo was taken?

3 How are the cities in the two photos different?

ACADEMIC WRITING SKILLS

WRITING A CONCLUDING SENTENCE

Some paragraphs have a concluding sentence. Usually, this sentence reminds the reader of the topic sentence. It can do this by restating the main idea, but with different words. It can also summarize the main points of the paragraph. Writers often add a concluding comment, such as their opinion or a prediction. Compare these topic sentences and concluding sentences:

Topic sentence: Since 2006, Masdar City has run into serious financial difficulties.

Concluding sentence: If all goes well, Masdar's green solutions to both traffic and environmental problems will outweigh the financial cost of building the city.

1 Read the paragraphs. Circle the best concluding sentence for each one. PRISM Online

Paragraph 1

Riding my bicycle to school has both advantages and disadvantages. The most important advantage is that it saves me time because I don't have to wait in traffic or spend time searching for a parking space. Cycling is great exercise, and it feels good. Also, cycling helps the environment because it does not create any pollution. However, there are two things I dislike about cycling. One is that it can be dangerous if drivers can't see you. Also, some drivers are very rude.

a In other words, some drivers think they own the road and cyclists have no place on it.
b Still, I think the advantages of cycling outweigh the disadvantages, and I will continue to use my bicycle to get around in good weather.
c Because of these disadvantages, I may sell my bike and take the bus.

Paragraph 2

In some cities, such as Seattle and Istanbul, people commute to work by ferry. A ferry carries people, and sometimes cars, over water between two or more places. Sometimes a ferry is the only way to get around because there are no roads or bridges. However, even if a road exists, many people prefer to travel by ferry because it saves time. Ferry passengers don't have to sit in traffic, and they can read or work on their computers. Another benefit is that ferries help the environment by keeping hundreds of cars and trucks off the roads.

a These advantages explain why people in cities all over the world travel to and from work by ferry.
b For me, the best thing about taking the ferry to work is that it is fun.
c Many ferries have a restaurant on board, and passengers can drink coffee or eat a meal while they commute.

ACADEMIC WRITING SKILLS 75

3 Writing

Critical thinking and production

Multiple critical thinking activities begin this section, preparing students for exercises that focus on grammar for writing and writing skills. All of these lead up to a structured writing task, in which students apply the skills and language they have developed over the course of the entire unit.

ON CAMPUS

COMMUNICATING WITH PROFESSORS

During their time at college, students need to communicate with their professors on a regular basis. The relationship that professors have with their students is different from a high-school teacher's relationship with their students, and it is important that students communicate with professors in the right way so that they have a positive and respectful relationship with them.

PREPARING TO READ

1 You are going to read an email exchange between a student and her professor. Before you read, work with a partner and discuss the questions.

1 Have you ever communicated with a professor or instructor outside of class? If so, how did you do it?
2 What are some reasons a student might contact a professor?
3 In your opinion, what is the best way to contact a professor outside of class?

 On Feb.12, David Alcott wrote:
To: Sunbaby123@mail.cup.com
Re: Hi
Dear Linda,
Please come see me tomorrow during my office hours.
Sincerely,
Professor Alcott

 On Feb 11, Linda Sun wrote:
hey dave–I had to miss the last few classes because of my work schedule. did i miss something important? can u send me the handouts and your presentation slides? i haven't been able to buy the book yet :(but i will get notes from someone else in the class.
Thanks!

100 UNIT 4

4 On Campus

Skills for college life

This unique section teaches students valuable skills beyond academic reading and writing. From asking questions in class to participating in a study group and from conducting research to finding help, students learn how to navigate university life. The section begins with a context-setting reading and moves directly into active practice of the skill.

WHAT MAKES *PRISM* SPECIAL: CRITICAL THINKING

Bloom's Taxonomy

In order to truly prepare for college coursework, students need to develop a full range of thinking skills. *Prism* teaches explicit critical thinking skills in every unit of every level. These skills adhere to the taxonomy developed by Benjamin Bloom. By working within the taxonomy, we are able to ensure that your students learn both lower-order and higher-order thinking skills.

Critical thinking exercises are accompanied by icons indicating where the activities fall in Bloom's Taxonomy.

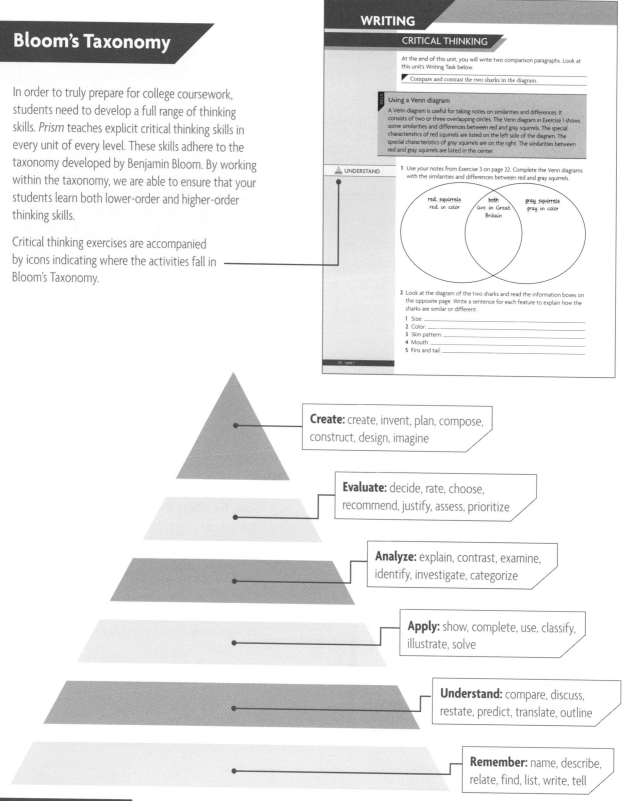

Create: create, invent, plan, compose, construct, design, imagine

Evaluate: decide, rate, choose, recommend, justify, assess, prioritize

Analyze: explain, contrast, examine, identify, investigate, categorize

Apply: show, complete, use, classify, illustrate, solve

Understand: compare, discuss, restate, predict, translate, outline

Remember: name, describe, relate, find, list, write, tell

WHAT MAKES *PRISM* SPECIAL: CRITICAL THINKING

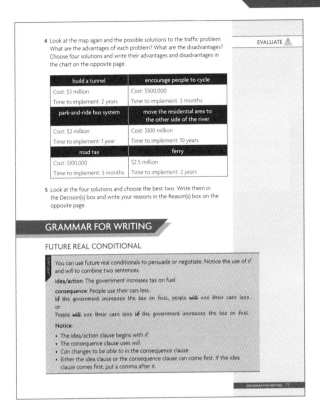

Higher-Order Thinking Skills

Create, **Evaluate**, and **Analyze** are critical skills for students in any college setting. Academic success depends on their abilities to derive knowledge from collected data, make educated judgments, and deliver insightful presentations. *Prism* helps students get there by creating activities such as categorizing information, comparing data, selecting the best solution to a problem, and developing arguments for a discussion or presentation.

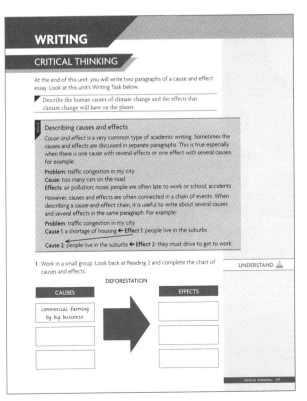

Lower-Order Thinking Skills

Apply, **Understand**, and **Remember** provide the foundation upon which all thinking occurs. Students need to be able to recall information, comprehend it, and see its use in new contexts. *Prism* develops these skills through exercises such as taking notes, mining notes for specific data, demonstrating comprehension, and distilling information from charts.

WHAT MAKES *PRISM* SPECIAL: ON CAMPUS

More college skills
Students need more than traditional academic skills. *Prism* teaches important skills for being engaged and successful all around campus, from emailing professors to navigating study groups.

Professors
Students learn how to take good lecture notes and how to communicate with professors and academic advisors.

Beyond the classroom
Skills include how to utilize campus resources, where to go for help, how to choose classes, and more.

Active learning
Students practice participating in class, in online discussion boards, and in study groups.

Texts
Learners become proficient at taking notes and annotating textbooks as well as conducting research online and in the library.

DISCUSSION

6 Work with a partner. Use information from Reading 1 and Reading 2 to answer the following questions.

SYNTHESIZING

1 As the world's climate changes, which places will have too much water? Which places will become drier? Give examples.
2 How do both the melting of the glaciers and deforestation contribute to the extinction of species?

⊚ LANGUAGE DEVELOPMENT

ACADEMIC VOCABULARY

1 Replace the underlined words in the sentences with the academic words in the box.

PRISM Online Workbook

| annual (adj)   areas (n)   challenge (n)   consequences (n) |
| contributes to (v)   issue (n)   predict (v)   trend (n) |

1 The most serious problem that threatens the environment is climate change. _____
2 Experts think that there will not be enough fresh water in the future. _____
3 Pollution and climate change are the effects of human activity. _____
4 Fortunately, we are seeing a pattern where people recycle more and use less packaging. _____
5 In some places, the glaciers have melted or even disappeared as a result of higher temperatures. _____
6 The yearly rate of species loss in the rainforest is nearly 50,000—that's 135 plant, animal, and insect species each day! _____
7 The biggest test we face is to protect the planet. _____
8 Human activity causes climate change. _____

LANGUAGE DEVELOPMENT 47

Vocabulary Research

Learning the right words

Students need to learn a wide range of general and academic vocabulary in order to be successful in college. *Prism* carefully selects the vocabulary that students study based on the General Service List, the Academic Word List, and the Cambridge English Corpus.

GRAMMAR FOR WRITING

VERBS OF CAUSE AND EFFECT

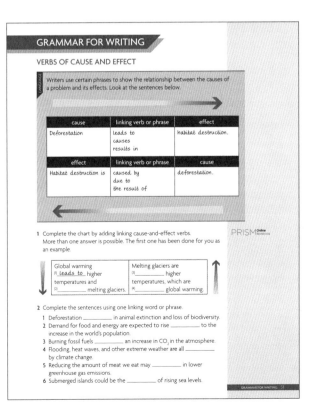

LANGUAGE

Writers use certain phrases to show the relationship between the causes of a problem and its effects. Look at the sentences below.

cause	linking verb or phrase	effect
Deforestation	leads to causes results in	habitat destruction.

effect	linking verb or phrase	cause
Habitat destruction is	caused by due to the result of	deforestation.

PRISM Online Workbook

1 Complete the chart by adding linking cause-and-effect verbs. More than one answer is possible. The first one has been done for you as an example.

| Global warming (1) *leads to* higher temperatures and (2)_____ melting glaciers. | Melting glaciers are (3)_____ higher temperatures, which are (4)_____ global warming. |

2 Complete the sentences using one linking word or phrase.

1 Deforestation _____ in animal extinction and loss of biodiversity.
2 Demand for food and energy are expected to rise _____ to the increase in the world's population.
3 Burning fossil fuels _____ an increase in CO_2 in the atmosphere.
4 Flooding, heat waves, and other extreme weather are all _____ by climate change.
5 Reducing the amount of meat we eat may _____ in lower greenhouse gas emissions.
6 Submerged islands could be the _____ of rising sea levels.

GRAMMAR FOR WRITING 51

Grammar for Writing

Focused instruction

This unique feature teaches learners the exact grammar they will need for their writing task. With a focus on using grammar to accomplish rhetorical goals, these sections ensure that students learn the most useful grammar for their assignment.

LEARNING OBJECTIVES

Reading skill	Read for main ideas
Grammar	Word order; Combining sentences with *and* and *or*, *but* and *whereas*, *both* and *neither*
Academic writing skill	Topic sentences
Writing Task	Complete a comparison and contrast essay
On Campus	Avoid plagiarism

ACTIVATE YOUR KNOWLEDGE

Work with a partner. Discuss the questions.

1 In your opinion, is it better to see animals in a zoo or in nature? Why?

2 Are there more wild animals in your country now, or were there more in the past? Why? Give examples.

3 Why do some people enjoy having animals in their homes?

4 Do humans need animals? Why or why not?

5 Are animals important in your life? Why?

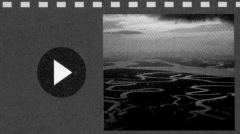   

PREPARING TO WATCH

1 You are going to watch a video about dolphins and egrets. Before you watch, work with a partner and discuss the questions.

1 What do you know about dolphins? Where do they live and what do they eat?

2 What do birds eat? How do they get their food?

2 Work with a partner. Look at the photos from the video and discuss the questions.

1 Why and when might dolphins come onto land?

2 Why do you think dolphins live in groups, rather than alone?

3 What is the relationship between the dolphins and the birds?

GLOSSARY

egret (n) a large white bird with long legs that lives near water

shore (n) the land beside an ocean, a lake, or a river

marsh (n) an area of soft, wet land

depend on (phr v) to need the help of someone or something in order to exist or continue as before

---

WHILE WATCHING

3 ▶ Watch the video. Number the sentences in order (1–5).

    a Young dolphins and egrets learn how to fish from their parents. _____

    b Dolphins and egrets live together in the marshes of South Carolina. _____

    c The dolphins' fishing technique helps the egrets get food. _____

    d The egrets watch the dolphins in the water carefully. _____

    e The dolphins push the fish onto land. _____

UNDERSTANDING MAIN IDEAS

4 ▶ Watch the video again. Write *T* (true), *F* (false), or *DNS* (does not say) next to the statements. Then, correct the false statements.

    _____ **1** The egrets are experts on the dolphins' behavior.

    _____

    _____ **2** The dolphins push the egrets onto the shore.

    _____

    _____ **3** When the fish are in the water, the dolphins start eating.

    _____

    _____ **4** The dolphins always use their left sides to push the fish.

    _____

    _____ **5** Some of the birds do not eat fish.

    _____

UNDERSTANDING DETAILS

DISCUSSION

5 Work in a small group. Discuss the questions. Then, compare your answers with another group.

    1 What other animals work together and help each other?

    2 Why would two different animals work together?

    3 What animals do humans work with? Why?

READING

PREPARING TO READ

UNDERSTANDING
KEY VOCABULARY

1 Read the definitions. Complete the sentences with the correct form
of the words in bold.

> **chemical** (n) man-made or natural substance made by changing atoms
> **destroy** (v) to damage something very badly; to cause it to not exist
> **due to** (prep) because of; as a result of
> **endangered** (adj) (of plants and animals) that may disappear soon
> **natural** (adj) as found in nature; not made or caused by people
> **pollute** (v) to make an area or substance dirty and unhealthful
> **protect** (v) to keep something or someone safe from damage or injury
> **species** (n) types of plants or animals that have similar features

1 The black rhino is one of the most _____ animals in the world.
   There are only about 5,000 left today.
2 There are three _____ of bears in North America. They are the
   American black bear, the grizzly bear, and the polar bear.
3 Dangerous _____ from factories can kill fish and other animals
   when they enter lakes and rivers.
4 Smoke from factories can _____ the air and hurt both humans
   and animals.
5 When new homes are built, it often _____ the areas where
   animals live.
6 Few people visited the zoo last week _____ the cold weather.
7 I don't like zoos. I prefer to see animals in their _____
   environments.
8 Many organizations are working to _____ endangered animals by
   creating safe places for them to live.

USING YOUR
KNOWLEDGE

2 Look at the title of the factsheet opposite. What do you think it will be
about? Complete the chart with the names of endangered and extinct
species you know.

endangered species	extinct species

3 Read the factsheet. Then, complete the chart with the names of animals mentioned in the factsheet.

Endangered Species

1   An **endangered species** is a group of animals or plants that could soon become extinct. Extinction happens when the last animal of the species has died out and there will be no more. Many species are nearly extinct and could disappear from the Earth very soon if we don't do anything to save them. There are many reasons why species become endangered, but most harm to species is **due to** human activities such as habitat destruction, hunting, and overfishing.

2   Habitat destruction is the main reason why animals become endangered. This happens in two ways. First, when humans move into a new area, they cut down trees to build houses and farms. This **destroys** the animals' habitat—the **natural** environment where plants or animals usually live—and leaves them without food. Animal habitats are also destroyed because of pollution. Dirty water from factories, which contains **chemicals**, ends up in rivers, and poisons used on farmland may even kill animals that live in the area.

3   Endangered species are also the result of hunting and fishing. Animals such as the Arabian oryx are nearly extinct because of the high price of their meat. Other animals are killed for their fur, bones, or skin—or just for sport. For example, some seal species are now almost extinct because they are killed for their fur to make coats. Tigers are shot to make medicine and tea from their bones, and crocodiles are caught to make bags and shoes. Large sea creatures like whales, tuna, and sharks have all become endangered species because of overfishing—too many are caught to make special dishes that people like to eat, such as shark's fin soup or sushi.

Arabian oryx

4   What steps can individuals and governments take to **protect** more animal and plant species from becoming endangered? We should try not to **pollute** natural areas, and farmers or companies who destroy animal habitats should face a financial penalty. The public can help out by refusing to buy products made from animals' body parts, such as seal fur coats or crocodile bags. Governments can help, too, by making it against the law to hunt, fish, or trade in endangered species. They can also provide funding for animal sanctuaries and zoos and protect animals from extinction by breeding more endangered animals, which can later be released into the wild. If we all cooperate by taking these steps, we will protect our planet so that our children and their children can enjoy it, too.

Reading for main ideas

The main idea of a paragraph tells the most important thought or message of that paragraph. The topic sentence expresses the main idea of the paragraph, and all of the other sentences in the paragraph give details to support the topic sentence. To find the main idea, look at the topic sentence and check whether the rest of the paragraph supports what it says.

READING FOR MAIN IDEAS

READING FOR DETAILS

4 Read the factsheet again and write the paragraph number next to the main ideas.

   a How hunting and overfishing endanger animals _____
   b The definition of endangered and extinct species _____
   c How governments and citizens can protect animals _____
   d How humans destroy and pollute animal habitats _____

5 Work with a partner. Answer the questions.

   1 Who or what is most responsible for animal extinction and endangered species?

   _____

   2 How does pollution and cutting down trees cause problems for animals?

   _____

   3 What do people hunt animals for?

   _____

   4 Which large sea creatures are endangered because of overfishing?

   _____

   5 What can individuals do to protect animals from becoming endangered?

   _____

   6 What should governments do about hunting and fishing of animals?

   _____

   7 What should governments invest in to get more animals back into the wild?

   _____

READING BETWEEN THE LINES

WORKING OUT MEANING

6 Read the last paragraph of the factsheet again and underline the words and phrases with the same meaning as the bold words.

   1 Companies who destroy animal habitats should **pay a fine**.
   2 You should help to protect animals by **choosing not to buy** fur.
   3 We can make it **illegal** to hunt, fish, or trade in endangered species.
   4 Governments can **pay for** animal sanctuaries and zoos.
   5 If we **work together** by **taking this action**, we can protect our planet.

DISCUSSION

7 Work with a partner. Discuss the questions.

1 What are some more examples of products that are made from animal parts? Do you use any of these products?
2 Should governments spend money to save animal habitats even if this means there is less money for things people need, such as hospitals?
3 Why is it a problem if some plants and animals die out?

READING 2

PREPARING TO READ

1 Read the definitions. Complete the sentences with the correct form of the words in bold.

UNDERSTANDING
KEY VOCABULARY

PRISM Online Workbook

> **common** (adj) happening often or existing in large numbers
> **cruel** (adj) causing pain or suffering on purpose
> **disease** (n) illness; a serious health condition that requires care
> **fatal** (adj) causing death
> **major** (adj) most serious or important
> **native** (adj) used to describe animals and plants that grow naturally in a place
> **survive** (v) to continue to live after almost dying

1 The coyote, a wild member of the dog family, is so _____ in the western United States that they can be seen in cities.
2 Plastic is often _____ to sea birds. Millions of birds die each year when they swallow plastic bags and other plastic garbage.
3 The flu is a common _____ in humans, but some animals, such as horses, birds, seals, and whales, can also get forms of the flu.
4 Many people believe that it is _____ to keep animals in zoos, where they can't move around freely.
5 Habitat loss is the _____ cause of species extinction in the Amazon River region.
6 Gray whales are endangered, but there is a chance that they will _____ because many countries have stopped hunting them.
7 There are many unique species that are _____ to the island of Madagascar, including more than 80 kinds of snakes.

2 Work with a partner. Look at the photos in the article on page 23 and discuss the questions.

PREDICTING CONTENT
USING VISUALS

1 What are the animals in the photos?
2 Do you have them in your country? How do people feel about them?
3 Which animal do you think is endangered? Why?

WHILE READING

3 Read the article and answer the questions.

READING FOR MAIN IDEAS

1 What is an invasive species?

_____

2 How did the gray squirrel enter Great Britain?

_____

3 How are the two species of squirrels similar?

_____

4 How are the two species of squirrels different?

_____

_____

5 What four reasons are given for the success of the gray squirrel in the U.K.?

_____

_____

SUMMARIZING

4 Read the summary and circle the correct words to complete it.

The article uses the example of the red and gray squirrel to explain what can happen when an invasive species competes with a native one. The [1]*gray / red* squirrel was introduced to Britain in the 19th century and has become very successful since then. Now there are [2]*fewer / more* than 140,000 native red squirrels left in the wild. The main reason why the gray squirrel is more successful is that it is [3]*fatter / thinner*, so it is less affected by cold weather. Another reason is that gray squirrels are [4]*unable / able* to live in cities. A further reason may be the parapox virus, which [5]*kills / injures* red squirrels. Even though many people regard the gray squirrel as a [6]*pest / pet*, [7]*most / few* British people support destroying gray squirrels. Because red squirrels [8]*are / aren't* endangered worldwide, perhaps they could be reintroduced to Great Britain.

READING BETWEEN THE LINES

MAKING INFERENCES

5 Read the article again and answer the questions.

1 Paragraph 1 mentions one way that nonnative species enter a new environment. What are some other ways?

_____

2 Why do you think gray squirrels are regarded as "major pests," other than the damage they do to plants and houses?

_____

3 What reason could some people give for trying to save the red squirrel?

_____

4 Why do you think there are no gray squirrels on the Isle of Wight?

_____

Losing the Battle for Survival

1 Invasive species are plants and animals that arrive in an area where they are not **native**, usually due to human activity. For example, a species of shellfish might attach itself to the outside of a ship traveling between countries and enter a new environment in this way. Invasive species are often able to grow quickly in their new homes because they have no natural enemies. As a result, they may replace or damage native plants and animals that live in the same environment. One example is the case of gray and red squirrels in Great Britain.

2 Red squirrels used to be a **common** sight in British forests and countryside. Then, in the 1870s, the gray squirrel was introduced from North America because rich people thought the squirrels looked fashionable in the grounds of their large homes. Today, only about 140,000 red squirrels remain, mostly in Scotland. In contrast, gray squirrels are now extremely common and seen as **major** pests due to the damage they cause to plants and houses. While red squirrels are protected, gray squirrels can be legally trapped and destroyed.

3 On first sight, the two species of squirrel are similar. They both have a long tail, which helps them balance when jumping from tree to tree, and the same large eyes, small ears, and powerful back legs.

4 In contrast, the two types of squirrel are different in body size and weight. The red squirrel has a typical head-and-body length of approximately 7.5 to 9 inches (19 to 23 centimeters), a tail length of 6 to 8 inches (15 to 20 centimeters) and a body weight of 9 to 12 ounces (250 to 340 grams). The gray squirrel is larger than the red squirrel. The head and body measure between 9 and 12 inches (23 and 30 centimeters), and the tail is between 7.5 and 10 inches (19 and 25 centimeters) long. Adult gray squirrels are also heavier, weighing between 14 and 21 ounces (400 and 600 grams). This size allows them to store more fat and helps them to **survive** hard winters, which could be **fatal** to their smaller cousins.

5 Three more differences explain why red squirrels have lost out in the competition with gray squirrels. First, red squirrels live high up in the trees, whereas gray squirrels spend more of their time on the ground. This means that any loss of forest habitat greatly affects the red squirrel population. Another reason is that gray squirrels are more intelligent and can adapt to new situations more easily than red squirrels. For example, they can survive in an urban environment because of their ability to use food provided by humans. A third problem for the red squirrel is **disease**. Both squirrels carry the parapox virus. The virus does not seem to affect gray squirrels, but it is fatal to reds.

6 In conclusion, there does not seem to be much that scientists can do to help red squirrels survive in Great Britain. Some politicians support destroying populations of gray squirrels, but many British people would contend that this is **cruel**. Red squirrels have been successfully reintroduced from other countries, and they could be protected in places where there are no gray squirrels, such as the Isle of Wight. However, some people question whether Britain should protect red squirrels at all. Worldwide, they are not an endangered species. Considering the evidence, saving the red squirrel may be a waste of British government money. Government conservation funding should instead be spent on other endangered animals.

DISCUSSION

6 Work with a partner. Use ideas from Reading 1 and Reading 2 to answer the following questions.

1 Which reasons in Reading 1 and Reading 2 explain why the red squirrel is an endangered species?
2 Which of the solutions in paragraph 6 of Reading 2 do you think could help to save the red squirrel from extinction? Why?
3 In your opinion, is trying to save British red squirrels a waste of time and money? Why or why not?
4 Are introduced animal or plant species a problem in your country? Why? Give examples.

◉ LANGUAGE DEVELOPMENT

ACADEMIC VERBS

PRISM Online Workbook

1 Read the sentences. Complete the definitions with the words in bold.

1 Tigers are an endangered species. If people continue to hunt them, it will be impossible for them to **survive**.
2 Very cold and snowy winters **affect** some animals, such as rabbits and squirrels, since they are unable to find food as easily.
3 Seabirds are often hurt due to oil spills. When that happens, biologists catch the birds, clean them, and then **release** them back to nature.
4 If we really want to save endangered species, governments and animal protection organizations need to **cooperate** and stop fighting each other.
5 Sometimes biologists catch endangered animals and **attach** a small radio to their bodies. Then, the biologists always know where the animals are.
6 In this paper, I intend to compare and **contrast** the appearance and behavior of Indian and African elephants.

a _____ (v) to work together for a particular purpose
b _____ (v) to influence or cause something to change
c _____ (v) to allow someone or something to leave a place
d _____ (v) to stay alive; to continue to exist, especially after an injury or threat
e _____ (v) to show or explain differences between two people, situations, or things
f _____ (v) to connect or join one thing to another

COMPARATIVE ADJECTIVES

LANGUAGE

When comparing things, the comparative form of the adjective is used. Use the comparative form of an adjective + *than* to compare two people or things.

Add *-er* to one-syllable adjectives. If the adjective ends in *-e*, just add *-r*.	The red squirrel is **smaller than** the gray squirrel. The gray squirrel is **larger than** the red squirrel.
Use *more/less* + adjective + *than* for adjectives with two or more syllables.	The gray squirrel is **more intelligent than** the red squirrel. The red squirrel is **less common than** the gray squirrel.
If an adjective with two syllables ends in *-y*, remove the *-y* and add *-ier*.	The gray squirrel is **heavier than** the red squirrel.

PRISM Online Workbook

2 Complete the sentences using the comparative form.

1 The red squirrel is smaller and _____ (weak) the gray squirrel.

2 Gray squirrels are generally _____ (healthy) their smaller cousins because grays are not affected by the parapox virus.

3 Gray squirrels are _____ (successful) red squirrels because they eat food provided by humans.

4 Red squirrels are _____ (endangered) gray squirrels, which are not at risk of extinction.

WRITING

CRITICAL THINKING

At the end of this unit, you will write two comparison paragraphs. Look at this unit's Writing Task below.

▸ Compare and contrast the two sharks in the diagram.

SKILLS

Using a Venn diagram

A Venn diagram is useful for taking notes on similarities and differences. It consists of two or three overlapping circles. The Venn diagram in Exercise 1 shows some similarities and differences between red and gray squirrels. The special characteristics of red squirrels are listed on the left side of the diagram. The special characteristics of gray squirrels are on the right. The similarities between red and gray squirrels are listed in the center.

▲ UNDERSTAND

1 Use your notes from Exercise 3 on page 22. Complete the Venn diagrams with the similarities and differences between red and gray squirrels.

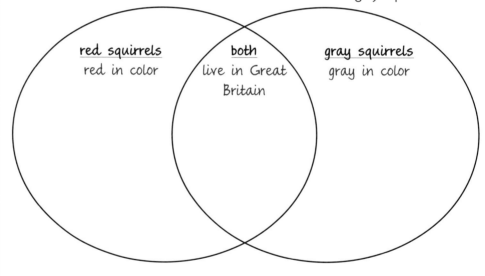

red squirrels
red in color

both
live in Great
Britain

gray squirrels
gray in color

2 Look at the diagram of the two sharks and read the information boxes on the opposite page. Write a sentence for each feature to explain how the sharks are similar or different.

1 Size: _____

2 Color: _____

3 Skin pattern: _____

4 Mouth: _____

5 Fins and tail: _____

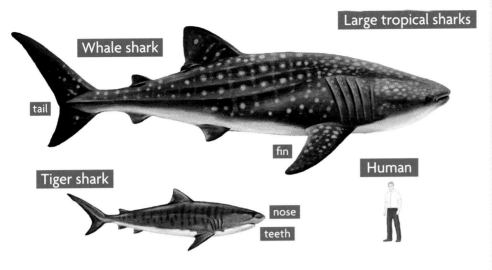

Large tropical sharks

Whale shark

tail

fin

Tiger shark

nose

teeth

Human

3 Look at more information about the two sharks and answer the questions.

Whale shark

Animal class: Chondrichthyes (fish)

Habitat: Oceans

Length: 18–32 feet (5.5–10 meters)

Weight: 40,000 pounds (20 tons)

Color: White belly, gray-blue back and sides with light spots

Diet: Plankton, krill, other very small animals

Conservation status: Endangered (will probably become extinct)

Behavior towards humans: No recorded attacks

Tiger shark

Animal class: Chondrichthyes (fish)

Habitat: Oceans

Length: 10–14 feet (3.0–4.2 meters)

Weight: 1900 pounds (0.95 tons)

Color: White belly, gray-brown back and sides

Diet: Tuna, dolphins, turtles

Conservation status: Not currently at risk of extinction

Behavior towards humans: 111 attacks since records began

1 Which shark is smaller?

_____

2 Which shark is heavier?

_____

3 Which shark eats large animals?

_____

4 Which shark eats tiny sea creatures?

_____

5 Which shark is in greater danger of extinction?

_____

6 Which shark is more dangerous to humans?

_____

4 Look at the diagram and read the information boxes on the previous page again. Complete the Venn diagram with information about the whale shark and the tiger shark.

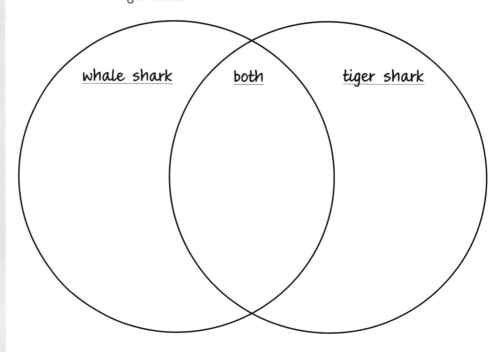

whale shark   both   tiger shark

GRAMMAR FOR WRITING

WORD ORDER

LANGUAGE

In English sentences, the subject usually comes before the verb and the object. These example sentences show other common features of English word order.

subject	verb	object
Squirrels	eat	seeds, nuts, and fruit.

subject	verb	adjective	prepositional phrase
Gray squirrels	are	common	in Britain.

linker	subject	verb	prepositional phrase
However,	they	were introduced	from North America.

1 Rewrite the words in the correct order.

1 lives / The tiger shark / in tropical oceans / .

_____

2 isn't / the whale shark / However, / dangerous / .

_____

3 The tiger shark / on its skin / markings / has / .

_____

4 a large mouth / and / has / The whale shark / plankton / eats / .

_____

COMBINING SENTENCES

and and *or*

When joining two sentences together, you can also take out some words. This makes the sentences shorter and better because you can avoid repetition.

In affirmative sentences, use *and*:

The tiger shark has sharp teeth. The tiger shark has a powerful bite.
→ The tiger shark has sharp teeth **and** a powerful bite.

In negative sentences, use *or*:

The whale shark does not have sharp teeth. The whale shark does not have a powerful bite. → The whale shark does not have sharp teeth **or** a powerful bite.

2 Join the pairs of sentences with *and* or *or*. Take out the repeated words.

1 The whale shark is gray-blue. The whale shark has light spots on its body.

_____ .

2 The tiger shark is gray-brown. The tiger shark has a striped pattern on its body.

_____ .

3 The tiger shark eats large sea creatures. The tiger shark can be dangerous to humans.

_____ .

4 The whale shark is not aggressive. The whale shark is not dangerous to swim with.

_____ .

5 The tiger shark is not an endangered species. The tiger shark is not a protected species.

_____ .

6 The whale shark is an endangered species. The whale shark is a protected species.

_____ .

but and whereas

But and *whereas* are used to contrast two sentences. *Whereas* is more formal than *but*.

The tiger shark has sharp teeth and a powerful bite, **but/whereas** the whale shark does not have sharp teeth or a powerful bite.

3 Look at the pairs of contrasting sentences you wrote in Exercise 2 and rewrite them using *but* or *whereas*.

1 _____

_____ .

2 _____

_____ .

3 _____

_____ .

both and neither

You can use other phrases to compare two different things.
If two things/people have the same characteristic, use *both ... and ...* :
Both the gray **and** red squirrel carry the parapox virus.

If they do not have a particular characteristic, use *neither ... nor ...* :
Neither the gray **nor** red squirrel is found in the north of Scotland.

PRISM Online Workbook

4 Write sentences using the information in the chart and *both ... and ...* or *neither ... nor ...* .

1 _____ .
2 _____ .
3 _____ .
4 _____ .
5 _____ .

	red squirrels	gray squirrels
1 have long tails	Yes	Yes
2 live on the Isle of Man	No	No
3 are meateaters	No	No
4 are an endangered species	No	No
5 live in forests	Yes	Yes

TOPIC SENTENCES

SKILLS

A **topic sentence** is usually the first sentence in a paragraph. It introduces the main idea of the paragraph and often the point that the writer wants to make about the topic. A topic sentence should be a general statement about the paragraph's subject, but it shouldn't be too specific. It is then supported by the other sentences in the paragraph.

Look at three topic sentences from paragraphs in Reading 2. Notice that both kinds of topic sentence refer to the <u>main essay topic</u> (the situation of red squirrels and gray squirrels in Great Britain).

A general statement
a On first sight, the two species of squirrel **are similar**.
b **Three more differences** explain why red squirrels have lost out in the competition with gray squirrels.

General statement + the topics of the supporting sentences
c In contrast, the two types of squirrel are different in **body size** and **weight**.

1 Look at the topic sentences (a–c) in the box above and at Reading 2 on page 23. Answer the questions.

1 Which sentences above introduce paragraphs about differences? _____ _____
2 Which sentence above introduces a paragraph about similarities? _____
3 In Reading 2, how many supporting sentences does each paragraph have? Are all the paragraphs the same length? What does this tell you about the "correct" number of sentences in a paragraph?

_____

_____

_____

2 In the following paragraph, the topic sentence is missing. Read the paragraph and the three possible topic sentences below it. Circle the letter of <u>two</u> possible topic sentences for the paragraph.

Both bear species are native to North America and are common in both the United States and Canada. Neither the black bear nor the grizzly bear is an endangered species. Despite their names, the species are also similar in color. "Black" bears can be black, brown, red, and even white. In the same way, grizzlies can range in color from black to blond. Finally, the two bear species are similar in behavior. They are intelligent, curious, and gentle unless humans enter their area or try to hurt their babies. Then both bears can become dangerous.

a Bears are one of the biggest attractions in the national parks of North America.
b The American black bear and the grizzly, or brown, bear are similar in many ways.
c The American black bear and the grizzly, or brown, bear are similar in habitat, color, and behavior.

WRITING TASK

Compare and contrast the two sharks in the diagram.

1 Review your notes in the Venn diagram you created in Exercise 4 in Critical Thinking.

WRITE A FIRST DRAFT

2 Read the introduction and the conclusion of the essay that compares and contrasts the two sharks. Complete the essay by writing two paragraphs about the differences in size, shape, color, diet, behavior, and conservation status between the two sharks. Refer to the Task Checklist on page 33 as you prepare your paragraphs.

The Whale Shark and the Tiger Shark

Introduction: The whale shark and the tiger shark are two of the many shark species found in the major oceans of the world. Both the whale shark and the tiger shark belong to the animal class Chondrichthyes. Both types of shark have a large mouth, a divided tail, and fins for swimming, including the large triangular fin that can often be seen above the surface of the water. On the other hand, these two types of shark are very different in their physical characteristics, diet, behavior, and conservation status.

Conclusion: Overall, it is clear that the whale shark is a much larger animal, but it is a gentle giant, whereas the smaller tiger shark is a hungry meateater. However, both animals play an important role in the ocean environment. For example, tiger sharks keep the oceans clean by eating dead whales and fish. In my opinion, people and nations need to cooperate to make sure we protect both of these important animal species.

REVISE

3 Use the Task Checklist to review your essay for content and structure.

TASK CHECKLIST	✔
Did you use a topic sentence to introduce each paragraph?	
Did you include information about the size, color, and weight of the two shark species?	
Did you include information about the diet, behavior, and conservation status of the two shark species?	

4 Make any necessary changes to your essay.

EDIT

5 Use the Language Checklist to edit your essay for language errors.

LANGUAGE CHECKLIST	✔
Did you use academic verbs correctly?	
Did you use comparative adjectives correctly?	
Did you use *and*, *or*, *but*, *whereas*, *neither*, and *both* correctly?	

6 Make any necessary changes to your essay.

AVOIDING PLAGIARISM

SKILLS

Plagiarism is taking other people's words and ideas and using them as your own. In North America, plagiarism is taken very seriously. Professors, librarians, and writing center tutors can all help you avoid plagiarism.

PREPARING TO READ

1 You are going to read a web article about plagiarism by three university staff. Before you read, work with a partner and discuss the questions.

   1 What are some reasons that students plagiarize?
   2 What happens in your school if a student plagiarizes?
   3 In your culture, is plagiarism different from North America? How?

Middleton University

HOME
ARTICLES
ALUMNI
ABOUT
CONTACT

Avoiding Plagiarism

Dee Mackey *Librarian*

Students are often confused about plagiarism. If something is not their own idea or their own work, they should cite[1] the source. That means they should say where they found something. When students cite a source, they always need to know the author and date of publication. They should also cite sources for photos and graphs. Generally, students should paraphrase information from others. That means students can use the ideas of another person, but they should use their own words. If they are unsure about anything, they should come and ask for help. We are happy to help them.

Dr. Moore *Professor of History*

Academic honesty is important in my class. If a student pretends that someone else's words are theirs, that's dishonest. If a student lets someone else write their paper, that's dishonest. And if they submit a paper that they used in another class, that's also dishonest. These are all examples of plagiarism.

The rules are simple: Do your own work, use your own words, and don't re-use your work. If students are having trouble, they should come see me. At our college, if a student plagiarizes, I have to report this to the Dean[2] of Students.

Jaye Evans *Writing Center Tutor*

Students often wait until the last minute, so they don't have time to write their paper. Then they go to the Internet and cut and paste things into their paper. That's never OK. I know and their professors know that they have copied. We can help students with their writing projects. That's why we are here. But they have to start early. We can't really help them at the last minute.

[1]**cite** (v) to mention something as an example or proof of something else
[2]**dean** (n) a head of a department or group at a college or university

WHILE READING

2 Read the web article and match the name of the speaker with their advice.

  1 Dee Mackey   **2** Dr. Moore   **3** Jaye Evans

  _____ _____   _____ _____   _____ _____

  a Paraphrase other people's words or ideas.
  b Get started early on a writing task.
  c Don't copy text from a website.
  d Don't turn in the same project for two different classes.
  e If an idea is from someone else, cite the source.
  f If a student plagiarizes, the university needs to know.

3 Read the web article again. Write _T_ (true) or _F_ (false) next to the statements. Correct the false statements.

  _____ **1** When students cut and paste from the Internet, it's not right, but no one will know.
  _____ **2** A student writer doesn't have to say where they got a photograph for their essay.
  _____ **3** The Writing Center wants students to come to them early.
  _____ **4** Students should cite their sources when they paraphrase.
  _____ **5** Having a friend write your paper is plagiarism.
  _____ **6** Professors don't want to help students with questions about plagiarism.

PRACTICE

4 Work in a small group. Discuss the questions.

  1 In the reading, what advice about plagiarism surprised you?
  2 From the reading, who would you prefer to ask for help? Why?
  3 Who would you ask for help at your school?

5 Write three do's and three don'ts based on the reading. Use your own words.

REAL-WORLD APPLICATION

6 Work with a partner. Interview three students or professors on your campus. Ask these questions:

  1 What is your advice to avoid plagiarism?
  2 Who are good people to ask for help about plagiarism questions?
  3 What is the punishment if you plagiarize?

7 Work with another pair. Use the answers from Exercise 6 to create a brochure with do's and don'ts for avoiding plagiarism and resources for getting help.

8 Share your brochure with the class.

LEARNING OBJECTIVES

Reading skill	Read for details
Grammar	Verbs of cause and effect; *because* and *because of*
Academic writing skill	Paragraph unity; supporting sentences and details
Writing Task	Complete a cause and effect essay
On Campus	Choose your courses

ACTIVATE YOUR KNOWLEDGE

Work with a partner. Discuss the questions.

1 Is the weather changing in your country? How?
2 What are some ways that humans have affected the environment?
3 What is the biggest environmental problem in your country?

  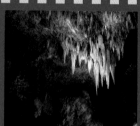 

PREPARING TO WATCH

1 You are going to watch a video about the natural environment. Before you watch, work with a partner and discuss the questions.

1 What are the Seven Natural Wonders of the World?

2 What are some important geographical features, like mountains or rivers, in your country?

3 What street or place names in your city or country refer to geography? (e.g., Pacific Coast Highway, Lake Street)

2 Work with a partner. Look at the photos from the video and discuss the questions.

1 Where are these places located?

2 How old do you think these places are?

3 Who owns these places?

GLOSSARY

canyon (n) a deep valley with very steep sides

form (v) to create; to make something begin to exist or take a particular shape

cavern (n) a large cave

spectacular (adj) extremely good, exciting, or beautiful

glacier (n) a large mass of ice that moves very slowly, usually down a slope or valley

---

WHILE WATCHING

3 ▶ Watch the video. Number the sentences in order (1–6).

> **a** The weather in the Grand Canyon can change very quickly. _____
> **b** Water is still changing the inside of Carlsbad Caverns. _____
> **c** Half Dome in Yosemite National Park was made by glaciers. _____
> **d** The Colorado River formed the Grand Canyon. _____
> **e** The rocks in the Grand Canyon are very old. _____
> **f** Yosemite Falls is the tallest waterfall in North America. _____

4 ▶ Watch the video again. Circle the correct answer.

1 The Grand Canyon was formed in _____ years.
   a a million
   b a few million
   c a billion
2 Some of the rocks in the Grand Canyon are _____ the Earth.
   a as old as
   b half as old as
   c almost as old as
3 The weather in the Grand Canyon can suddenly change from _____ .
   a hot to dry
   b dry to wet
   c hot to cold
4 The Carlsbad Caverns is the _____ cave system in North America.
   a oldest
   b largest
   c widest
5 The water in Yosemite National Park comes from _____ .
   a snow
   b glaciers
   c a cave

DISCUSSION

5 Work in a small group. Discuss the questions. Then, compare your answers with another group.

1 How might water change the Earth's geography in the next 100 years?
2 Do you think that glaciers will ever return to where you live?
3 Who should protect special natural areas in the world?

PREPARING TO READ

1 You are going to read a Web page about climate change. Before you read the web page, read the sentences below. Complete the definitions with the words in bold.

1 The Amazon rainforest is one of the largest **ecosystems** in the world. It is home to more than 10% of all the known plants and animals on Earth.

2 Southern California has a very pleasant **climate**. The winters are not too cold and the summers are not too hot.

3 Pesticides—chemicals generally used to kill insects that damage plants—also **threaten** helpful insects, such as bees.

4 In order to fight pollution, scientists are developing car engines that use electric or solar energy instead of **fossil fuels** like gasoline.

5 Methane (CH4) is a **greenhouse gas** that is found naturally inside the Earth and under the sea. It is used for cooking and heating homes and buildings.

6 The Earth's **atmosphere** is 300 miles (480 km) thick and contains a mixture of about 10 different gases, which we call *air*.

7 Because of **global warming**, polar ice is melting, sea levels are rising, and some islands might soon be underwater.

8 Habitat loss is the most important **cause** of species extinction.

a _____ (n) a gas that makes the air around the Earth warmer

b _____ (n) someone or something that makes something happen

c _____ (n) the layer of gases around the Earth

d _____ (n) the general weather conditions usually found in a particular place

e _____ (n) an increase in the Earth's temperature because of pollution

f _____ (v) to be likely to damage or harm something

g _____ (n) all the living things in an area and the effect they have on each other and the environment

h _____ (n) a source of energy like coal, gas, and petroleum, that was formed inside the Earth millions of years ago

2 Work with a partner. Look at the photo of the Upsala glacier and discuss the questions.

1 What has happened to the glacier?

2 What caused this transformation?

3 What are some other places where a similar transformation is happening today?

4 How do you think this will affect the world?

Our
Changing Planet

The Upsala glacier in Argentina used to be one of the biggest glaciers in South America. In 1928, it was covered in ice and snow, but now the glacier is melting at an annual rate of about 650 feet (about 200 meters), so the area is covered in water. This is evidence of **global warming**.

1 In the last 100 years, the global temperature has gone up by around 1.33 degrees Fahrenheit (0.75 degrees Celsius). This may not sound like much, but such a small increase is causing sea levels to rise and **threatening** the habitat of many species of plants and animals. An increase of 3.6 degrees Fahrenheit (2 degrees Celsius) in global temperatures could result in extinction for 30% of the world's land species.

2 The Northwest Passage is a sea route that runs along the northern coast of Canada between the Atlantic and the Pacific Oceans. In the past, it was often difficult to use because the water was frozen; however, increasing temperatures and the subsequent deglaciation[1] have made it easier for ships to travel through this route. The trouble is that the melting of the ice will lead to loss of habitat for the polar bears and other species that live in this area.

3 Experts predict that global sea levels could rise by 12 to 48 inches (30.5–122 centimeters) by the end of the century. Consequently, some areas that were land a few hundred years ago are now underwater, and many low-lying islands may be under water in the future.

4 As a result of the changing **climate**, the world's **ecosystems** are also changing faster than ever before. More than one-third of the world's mangrove forests[2] and around 20% of the world's coral reefs[3] have been destroyed in the last few decades. Forests are being cut down to provide land for food because human population is growing at such a rapid rate. Approximately a quarter of the land on Earth is now used for growing food. As a result of the higher temperatures and higher levels of carbon dioxide in the **atmosphere**, plants are producing more pollen, which could lead to more cases of asthma, a medical condition that makes it hard to breathe.

5 What is causing climate change? The main **cause** is the huge amount of **greenhouse gases**, such as methane and carbon dioxide (CO_2), in the atmosphere, but the reason for this is the world's population—you and me. As the population increases, more land is needed to provide food and energy. Burning **fossil fuels** for heating, lighting, transportation, electricity, or manufacturing produces CO_2. Furthermore, humans breathe out CO_2 while trees "breathe in" CO_2 and produce oxygen, so by cutting down trees, we are increasing the amount of CO_2 in the atmosphere and reducing the amount of oxygen. As a result of human activities, CO_2 levels are now at their highest in 800,000 years.

6 The biggest challenge we all face is to prevent further environmental disasters. We must do something before it is too late. We need to reduce the amount of CO_2 in the atmosphere. We need to stop burning fossil fuels and start using renewable energy. We can get enough energy from renewable fuels such as solar energy, hydroelectric energy, or wind power to be able to stop using fossil fuels completely.

Sign the petition to tell governments to take action before it is too late!

[1]**deglaciation** (n) the melting of a glacier
[2]**mangrove forest** (n) large areas of trees and shrubs that live in coastal areas, e.g., in Florida and Bangladesh
[3]**coral reefs** (n) diverse underwater ecosystems built by tiny animals

WHILE READING

3 Read the Web page and number the main ideas in the order that they are mentioned.

solution to the problem _____

changing ecosystems _____

melting glaciers _____

causes of climate change _____

4 Read the Web page again. Complete the sentences using the words and phrases in the box.

> CO_2 levels   coral reefs   extinction   farming
> global sea levels   global temperatures   mangrove forests

1 Over the last century, _____ have gone up by 0.75 degrees Celsius.

2 Global increases in temperature could cause the _____ of 30% of land species.

3 _____ could rise by about 12 inches by the end of the century.

4 Recently, over a third of the world's _____ have been destroyed.

5 Twenty percent of the Earth's _____ have been lost in the last few decades.

6 Twenty-five percent of the land on Earth is used for _____ .

7 _____ are at their highest for 800,000 years.

SKILLS

Reading for details

In a paragraph, the sentences that come after the topic sentence contain *supporting details*—information to help the reader understand the main idea more fully. Types of supporting details include facts, statistics, examples, reasons, explanations, comparisons, and descriptions.

Often, the topic sentence includes words that tell you what type of supporting sentences to expect in the body of the paragraph. For example:

Topic sentence: What is causing climate change?

The words *is causing* tell you that the paragraph will use causes, or reasons, to explain the main idea.

5 Read the Web page again and complete the chart with supporting details.

1 country where the Upsala glacier is located	
2 name of sea route through the arctic ice	
3 why forests are being cut down all over the world	
4 medical problem caused by pollen	
5 main chemicals responsible for climate change	
6 human activities that reduce the amount of O_2 in the atmosphere	
7 what should be done to reduce the amount of CO_2 in the atmosphere	

READING BETWEEN THE LINES

6 Why did the author write the Web page? Circle the correct answer.

   a To inform the reader about the causes of melting glaciers
   b To educate the reader about how to stop climate change
   c To convince people to sign a petition about using renewable fuels

DISCUSSION

7 Work with a partner. Discuss the questions.

   1 Are there any advantages to the melting of the glaciers in the Northwest Passage? Explain your answer.
   2 What are the possible disadvantages of using renewable energy like solar energy or wind power?
   3 Why don't governments, corporations, and individuals do more to help prevent global warming?

PREPARING TO READ

1 You are going to read an essay about deforestation. Before you read, look at the photo and the title of the essay. Then, answer the questions.

1 Why are trees important for the environment?

_____

2 Why do people cut down trees?

_____

3 What will happen if we destroy too many trees?

_____

_____

2 Read the definitions. Complete the sentences with the correct form of the words in bold.

---

absorb (v) to take in a liquid or gas through a surface and hold it
construction (n) the process of building something, usually large structures such as houses, roads, or bridges
destruction (n) the act of causing so much damage to something that it stops existing because it cannot be repaired
effect (n) result; a change that happens because of a cause
farming (n) the job of working on a farm or organizing work on a farm
logging (n) the activity or business of cutting down trees for wood
rainforest (n) a forest in a tropical area that gets a lot of rain

---

1 Clothes made from plants, like cotton or bamboo, _____ water more easily than man-made materials like polyester.

2 _____ has been the occupation of my family since my grandfather bought his first cow 75 years ago.

3 _____ hurts native people because it destroys the forest that provides them with food, shelter, and medicine.

4 The Amazon _____ in South America receives 60 to 118 inches (150 to 300 centimeters) of rain every year.

5 Because of heavy snow, the _____ of the new road stopped for more than two months.

6 Sunburn is just one of the harmful _____ of too much sun on sensitive skin.

7 Hurricane Katrina in 2005 caused serious _____ along the U.S. coast from Florida to Texas and killed more than 1,800 people.

The Causes and Effects of Deforestation

1   Forests, which cover almost one-third of the surface of the Earth, produce oxygen and provide homes to plants, animals, and humans. These days, many of the world's great forests are threatened by *deforestation*: the process of removing trees from large areas of land. The **destruction** of forests occurs for several reasons: Trees are used as fuel or for **construction**, and cleared land is used as pasture[1] for animals and fields for planting food. The main harmful **effects** of deforestation are climate change and damage to animal habitats.

2   The main causes of deforestation are commercial **farming** by big business and farming by local people. Huge commercial farms have taken over large areas of forest in many countries. In Indonesia, for example, industrial **logging** is carried out to clear huge areas for the production of palm oil, while in Brazil, large areas of the Amazon **rainforest** are cleared to grow soy and vegetable oil. In contrast, local farmers may cut down and burn trees to clear an area just big enough to graze cattle or grow crops. However, after two or three years, the land can no longer be used, so the farmer moves to another piece of land. Normally, it takes around ten years for cleared land to recover, but in populated areas, the land is never allowed to recover. This constant reuse of land leads to heavy erosion—the loss of the top layer of soil that protects the ground. Erosion, in turn, can cause flooding in heavy rain.

3   One serious effect of deforestation is climate change. Normally tropical rainforests help control the Earth's temperature by **absorbing** carbon dioxide. As an example, the vast rainforest of the Amazon covers an area of more than 2.6 million square miles—about 10 times the size of Texas—and absorb an estimated 1.5 billion tons of carbon dioxide annually. However, in areas where deforestation has taken place, the carbon dioxide goes into the atmosphere and traps heat in a process called the *greenhouse effect*. The result is global warming. Increasing global temperatures result in less rain. This causes the rainforests to dry out and leads to fires—which cause more emissions of carbon dioxide. In this way, the rainforests actually contribute to global warming instead of helping to solve it.

4   Forest destruction also has an effect on biodiversity[2]. Deforestation causes the loss of habitats and damage to land where plants and animal species live, leading to the extinction of many species. A decrease in biodiversity threatens entire ecosystems and destroys future sources of food and medicine.

5   In conclusion, damage to the world's forests is leading to changes in the natural environment and causing global warming. Looking to the future, governments should act to plant more trees that will absorb carbon dioxide and protect forests from illegal logging. Otherwise, deforestation on such a large scale is sure to have terrible effects on the environment.

[1] **pasture** (n) an area of land with grass for animals to eat
[2] **biodiversity** (n) the variety of different animals and plants in an area

WHILE READING

3 Read the essay and complete the summary using the words in the box.

> animals crops decade deforestation effects
> environment erosion habitats protected warming

The essay discusses the human causes of (1)_____ and the (2)_____ on the environment. Trees are removed for grazing of (3)_____ and growing (4)_____ like soy and palm oil. Farmers traditionally leave the land for a (5)_____ before reusing it, but if the land is constantly reused, it results in (6)_____ of the soil. Deforestation allows CO_2 to escape into the atmosphere and contributes to global (7)_____ . It also affects biodiversity because it leads to the loss of (8)_____ . Governments should make sure forests are (9)_____ from logging. Otherwise, deforestation will have terrible consequences for the (10)_____ .

4 Read the essay again and correct the factual mistakes in the sentences.

1 In Indonesia, trees are cut down to make way for olive oil plantations.

_____

2 Farmers can graze animals on their land for ten years.

_____

3 The rainforests of the Amazon cover an area 10 times the size of the U.S.

_____

4 Deforestation protects future sources of food and medicine.

_____

5 Governments should plant more trees to absorb oxygen.

_____

6 Small-scale deforestation will have disastrous effects on the environment.

_____

READING BETWEEN THE LINES

5 Work with a partner. Answer the questions.

1 What does the writer mean by the phrases *industrial logging* and *commercial farming?*

_____

2 What will probably happen if the Amazon rainforest disappears?

_____

3 Why does deforestation reduce future sources of food and medicine?

_____

DISCUSSION

6 Work with a partner. Use information from Reading 1 and Reading 2 to answer the following questions.

1 As the world's climate changes, which places will have too much water? Which places will become drier? Give examples.
2 How do both the melting of the glaciers and deforestation contribute to the extinction of species?

⊘ LANGUAGE DEVELOPMENT

ACADEMIC VOCABULARY

1 Replace the underlined words in the sentences with the academic words in the box.

PRISM Online Workbook

> annual (adj)   areas (n)   challenge (n)   consequences (n)
> contributes to (v)   issue (n)   predict (v)   trend (n)

1 The most serious <u>problem</u> that threatens the environment is climate change. _____
2 Experts <u>think</u> that there will not be enough fresh water in the future. _____
3 Pollution and climate change are the <u>effects</u> of human activity. _____
4 Fortunately, we are seeing a <u>pattern</u> where people recycle more and use less packaging. _____
5 In some <u>places</u>, the glaciers have melted or even disappeared as a result of higher temperatures. _____
6 The <u>yearly</u> rate of species loss in the rainforest is nearly 50,000—that's 135 plant, animal, and insect species each day! _____
7 The biggest <u>test</u> we face is to protect the planet. _____
8 Human activity <u>causes</u> climate change. _____

ENVIRONMENT COLLOCATIONS

2 Match the nouns to make collocations about the environment.

1	climate	**a**	group
2	environmental	**b**	plant
3	tropical	**c**	change
4	carbon	**d**	gas
5	power	**e**	rainforest
6	natural	**f**	resource
7	greenhouse	**g**	dioxide

3 Complete the sentences with the correct form of the collocations from Exercise 2.

1 In my town, about 70% of the electricity comes from a
_____ that uses coal for energy.

2 Carbon dioxide and methane are examples of _____ .

3 Almost all scientists these days agree that _____ is
happening and it is a serious threat to our planet.

4 Trees absorb _____ and give off oxygen.

5 All over the world, _____ are working to educate
people about the dangers of deforestation and habitat destruction.

6 Fresh water is the most precious _____ on Earth.

7 Thousands of unique plants, animals, birds, and insects live in the
_____ of South America and Southeast Asia.

WRITING

CRITICAL THINKING

At the end of this unit, you will write two paragraphs of a cause and effect essay. Look at this unit's Writing Task below.

> Describe the human causes of climate change and the effects that climate change will have on the planet.

Describing causes and effects

Cause and effect is a very common type of academic writing. Sometimes the causes and effects are discussed in separate paragraphs. This is true especially when there is one cause with several effects or one effect with several causes. For example:

Problem: traffic congestion in my city
Cause: too many cars on the road
Effects: air pollution; noise; people are often late to work or school; accidents

However, causes and effects are often connected in a chain of events. When describing a cause-and-effect chain, it is useful to write about several causes and several effects in the same paragraph. For example:

Problem: traffic congestion in my city
Cause 1: a shortage of housing ← **Effect 1**: people live in the suburbs

Cause 2: people live in the suburbs ← **Effect 2**: they must drive to get to work

1   Work in a small group. Look back at Reading 2 and complete the chart of causes and effects.

UNDERSTAND ▲

DEFORESTATION

CAUSES		EFFECTS
commercial farming by big business	→	

2 Read paragraph 3 of Reading 2 again. Complete the cause-and-effect chain with items from the box.

less rain	more CO_2 emissions	fires
global warming	forests dry out	CO_2 enters atmosphere and traps heat (greenhouse effect)

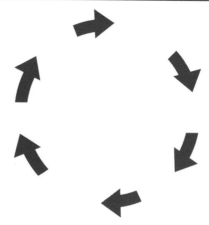

APPLY

3 Using information from Reading 1 and Reading 2 as well as your own ideas, brainstorm the human causes and effects of climate change.

4 Complete the charts with your ideas from Exercise 3. Make sure to include at least three causes.

CLIMATE CHANGE

CAUSES	EFFECTS

GRAMMAR FOR WRITING

VERBS OF CAUSE AND EFFECT

Writers use certain phrases to show the relationship between the causes of a problem and its effects. Look at the sentences below.

cause	linking verb or phrase	effect
Deforestation	leads to causes results in	habitat destruction.

effect	linking verb or phrase	cause
Habitat destruction is	caused by due to the result of	deforestation.

1 Complete the chart by adding linking cause-and-effect verbs. More than one answer is possible. The first one has been done for you as an example.

Global warming (1) _leads to_ higher temperatures and (2)_____ melting glaciers.	Melting glaciers are (3)_____ higher temperatures, which are (4)_____ global warming.

2 Complete the sentences using one linking word or phrase.

1 Deforestation _____ in animal extinction and loss of biodiversity.

2 Demand for food and energy are expected to rise _____ to the increase in the world's population.

3 Burning fossil fuels _____ an increase in CO_2 in the atmosphere.

4 Flooding, heat waves, and other extreme weather are all _____ by climate change.

5 Reducing the amount of meat we eat may _____ in lower greenhouse gas emissions.

6 Submerged islands could be the _____ of rising sea levels.

BECAUSE AND BECAUSE OF

Because is a conjunction that introduces a reason. It is followed by a subject, a verb, and sometimes an object.

The environment is changing **because** humans are burning fossil fuels.

Because of is a two-word preposition meaning "as a result of." It is followed by a noun phrase (made up of articles, adjectives, and nouns).

The climate is changing **because of** human activity.

PRISM Online Workbook

3 Complete the sentences using *because* or *because of*.

1 Sea levels may rise _____ melting glaciers.
2 In a warmer world, there are more fires _____ there is less rain.
3 The atmosphere is becoming warmer _____ deforestation and burning fossil fuels.
4 Low-lying islands may be submerged _____ sea levels are rising.

ACADEMIC WRITING SKILLS

PARAGRAPH UNITY

A well-written paragraph has just one main idea, and all the supporting sentences in the paragraph should explain or give information about it. They should not introduce any new topics.

When a paragraph has these characteristics, it has **unity**. Unity is a basic requirement of good academic writing.

PRISM Online Workbook

1 In the paragraph, circle the main idea. Then, cross out one sentence that does not support that idea.

Bottled Water

Do you drink water from plastic bottles? If you do, you might want to think about changing your habit because plastic water bottles hurt both people and the environment. First of all, plastic bottles contain two harmful chemicals, BPA and phthalates. Both types of chemicals can cause serious health problems in both adults and children. Second, plastic bottles hurt the environment. The bottles are made from petroleum, and transporting them requires an enormous amount of polluting fossil fuels. In the 1970s, the United States was the world's biggest exporter of fossil fuels. Also, most plastic bottles are not recycled. They end up in our landfills, where they can take many decades to break down. Because of these harmful effects of plastic water bottles on people and the environment, I have stopped buying them. I now drink water from the faucet, and guess what: It tastes good!

SUPPORTING SENTENCES AND DETAILS

Good writers use **supporting sentences** to develop and explain the main idea of a paragraph. The supporting sentences state important points about the main idea. Normally, writers provide **details**—facts, examples, reasons, or explanations—for each supporting point in a paragraph.

Look at the outline of a paragraph from Reading 2. Notice the kinds of details it includes.

Topic sentence: *The main causes of deforestation are commercial farming by big business and farming by local people.*

1ˢᵗ supporting sentence: *Huge commercial farms have taken over large areas of forest in many countries.*

Details (examples): *In Indonesia, for example, industrial logging is carried out to clear huge areas for the production of palm oil, while in Brazil, large areas of the Amazon rainforest are cleared to grow soy and vegetable oil.*

2ⁿᵈ supporting sentence: *In contrast, local farmers may cut down and burn trees to clear an area just big enough to graze cattle or grow crops.*

Details (facts/explanation): *However, after two or three years, the land can no longer be used, so the farmer moves to another piece of land. Normally, it takes around ten years for cleared land to recover, but in populated areas, the land is never allowed to recover.*

Details (reasons): *This constant reuse of land leads to heavy erosion—the loss of the top layer of soil that protects the ground. Erosion, in turn, can cause flooding in heavy rain.*

2 Read the paragraph *Bottled Water* on the opposite page again and answer the questions.

1 Find two supporting sentences and underline them.

2 What detail is given to explain the first supporting sentence? Is this a fact, example, or reason?

_____

3 How do plastic bottles harm the environment, according to the paragraph? What details does the paragraph include to explain each effect—facts, examples, or reasons?

_____

_____

_____

Describe the human causes of climate change and the effects that climate change will have on the planet.

PLAN

1 Look at the chart and cause-and-effect chain you created in Exercise 4 in Critical Thinking.

2 Look at the structure of the essay on page 45 as you plan your essay.

3 Refer to the Task Checklist on page 55 as you prepare your paragraphs.

WRITE A FIRST DRAFT

4 Read the introduction and conclusion of the cause and effect essay. Complete the introduction paragraph by writing two or three causes of climate change that you will discuss in your body paragraphs.

5 Then, complete the essay by writing two body paragraphs: one about the human causes of climate change and another about the effects. Remember to list the two or three causes you mentioned in the introduction.

Causes and Effects of Climate Change

Introduction: The Earth's climate has changed several times throughout history. According to the National Aeronautics and Space Administration (NASA), there have been seven cycles of warming and cooling in the last 650,000 years. These earlier cycles occurred naturally as a result of changes in the atmosphere. In contrast, nearly all climate scientists agree that the climate changes we are seeing today are caused by human activities, especially _____ , and these activities are having serious negative effects on our planet.

Conclusion: To conclude, human activity is clearly causing the climate to change and, as a result, the planet is experiencing a number of negative effects. It is important that we reduce our negative impact on the planet as much as possible—for example, by using renewable energy instead of fossil fuels—before it is too late.

REVISE

6 Use the Task Checklist to review your essay for content and structure. If you have any problems with content, look back at the Critical Thinking section.

TASK CHECKLIST	✔
Did you include two or three causes and effects from your notes in the Critical Thinking section?	
Did you use a suitable topic sentence for each paragraph?	
Does each paragraph include supporting sentences?	
Does each paragraph have unity?	
Did you include facts, examples, or reasons to explain each supporting sentence?	

7 Make any necessary changes to your essay.

EDIT

8 Use the Language Checklist to edit your essay for language errors.

LANGUAGE CHECKLIST	✔
Did you use the correct collocations for the environment?	
Did you use verbs of cause and effect correctly?	
Did you use *because* and *because of* correctly?	
Did you use the correct tenses, nouns, and adjectives?	

9 Make any necessary changes to your essay.

CHOOSING YOUR COURSES

 SKILLS Each semester or quarter, college students must register for new courses. There are a lot of classes to choose from, so students need to take time to choose courses carefully and understand the different types of courses in their program.

PREPARING TO READ

1 You are going to read a Web page about course information for students who are studying business. Before you read, work with a partner and discuss the questions.

    1 What subject do you want to study at college? Why?

    2 What other subjects are interesting to you? Why?

    3 What kinds of courses do you think will be most difficult? Why?

    4 Do you have experience choosing your own college classes? Who would be a good person to help you choose your classes?

○ ● ●

WEST FALLS COLLEGE
School of Business

COURSE OFFERINGS FOR FIRST YEAR BUSINESS MAJORS

Course Schedules are available online October 14. Registration for Winter Quarter opens November 4.

All students should make an appointment with their Academic Advisor before registration.

International students must be full-time and take 12 or more credits[1]. Except for summer quarter.

WINTER QUARTER COURSES

REQUIRED COURSES[2]

- Math 124 – Calculus (3 credits) Prerequisite[3]: Math 123
- Economics 202 – Microeconomics (3 credits)
- Management 200 – Basics of Management (3 credits)

Business majors only

ELECTIVES[4]

- Psychology 210 – Human Behavior (4 credits)
- Sociology 115 – Social Problems (3 credits)
- Communications 110 – Intercultural Communications (3 credits)

 Special

SUMMER COURSES

Register early for these popular electives! Information meeting dates

- Study Abroad, London (3 credits) – October 31
- Business Internship (2 credits) – November 5
- Service Learning (3 credits) – November 8

[1]**credit** (n) unit of measure for a college course

[2]**required courses** (n) courses that students must take for a degree

[3]**prerequisite** (n) a course that students must take before another class

[4]**electives** (n) courses related to a major that students can choose to take based on their interests

WHILE READING

2 Read the Web page. Complete the sentences with the correct words or
phrases. There are three extra options.

> advisor   electives   prerequisites   professor
> required courses   schedule   summer courses   time

1 Students should make an appointment with their
_____ before they register for classes.
2 Students must take all of the _____ for a degree.
3 Sometimes a course will have _____ , so students
have to take those classes first.
4 Students choose _____ that are related to their
major and their interests.

3 Read the Web page again. Write *T* (true) or *F* (false) next to the
statements. Correct the false statements.

_____ 1 Any student at the college can take Management 200.
_____ 2 In the summer, students can study in another country.
_____ 3 Business majors must take Sociology 115.
_____ 4 International students don't have to be full-time in the summer.
_____ 5 Many students like to take the Special Summer Programs.
_____ 6 All classes have the same number of credits.

PRACTICE

4 Imagine you are a business student at West Falls College. Choose your
courses for the Winter Quarter from the reading. Your schedule should
be full-time (at least 12 credits) and should include a required course and
an elective.

REAL-WORLD APPLICATION

5 Visit the website of your school or a school you want to go to and
search for your major.

1 Find the requirements for your major.
2 Find the electives for your major.
3 Find the Course Schedule for the next semester or quarter.
4 Create a chart with your class schedule of 15–18 credits. Include the
name of each class, how many credits it is worth and the time of
the class.

6 Work in a small group and share your information.

LEARNING OBJECTIVES

Reading skill	Predict content using visuals
Grammar	Future real conditionals; *if ... not* and *unless*
Academic writing skill	Write a concluding sentence
Writing Task	Complete a problem-solution essay
On Campus	Create idea maps

TRANSPORTATION

ACTIVATE YOUR KNOWLEDGE

1 Work with a partner. Look at the photo. How many different types of transportation can you name?

2 Which modes of transportation do you use? Answer the questions.
   1 Why do you use these modes of transportation?
   2 Why do you not use the other modes of transportation?

PREPARING TO WATCH

ACTIVATING YOUR
KNOWLEDGE

1 You are going to watch a video about airplanes. Before you watch, work with a partner and discuss the questions.

1 What is the biggest airplane you have ever been on?
2 What is the longest flight you have ever taken?
3 How many hours do you think an airplane can fly without stopping?

PREDICTING CONTENT
USING VISUALS

2 Work with a partner. Look at the photos from the video and discuss the questions.

1 How old do you think this airplane is?
2 What did people probably use the room in the fourth picture for?
3 What are the differences between first class and regular/coach class on airplanes today?

GLOSSARY
jumbo jet (n) a very large airplane that can carry hundreds of passengers
straight (adv) following one after the other without stopping
lounge (n) a room in a hotel, theater, airport, etc. where people can relax or wait
turn into (phr v) to make something change or become something different

WHILE WATCHING

3 ▶ Watch the video. Complete the summary with the words in the box.

| changed | flew | had | helped | worked |

    In 1969, the 747 (1)_____ across the Atlantic Ocean. Jimmy Barber
(2)_____ build the first 747. He and his team (3)_____ for many
hours a day to complete it. The first 747 (4)_____ two floors, with a
lounge on the second floor. The 747 (5)_____ air travel forever.

4 ▶ Watch the video again. Circle the correct answer.

1 The ability to carry enough _____ changed air travel.
   a people   **b** fuel   **c** baggage

2 Today, many airplanes can travel for _____ hours without stopping.
   a 8   **b** 12   **c** 14

3 The first 747s could carry about _____ people.
   a 500   **b** 747   **c** 1,000

4 In 1969, the 747 was the most _____ plane in the world.
   a modern   **b** expensive   **c** famous

5 The _____ of air travel today is much lower than it was 50 years ago.
   a cost   **b** speed   **c** comfort

DISCUSSION

5 Work in a small group. Discuss the questions.

  1 What are the advantages of air travel?
  2 What are the disadvantages of air travel?

6 Complete the chart with one advantage and one disadvantage for each
kind of transportation with your group. Then, compare your answers with
another group.

transportation	advantage	disadvantage
1 car		
2 train		
3 bus		
4 bike		
5 boat		

READING

PREPARING TO READ

SKILLS

Predicting content using visuals

The images that accompany a text can provide valuable information about the content. For example, they can tell you where the text is set, what it is about, what kind of text it is (essay, blog post, etc.), what the key points are, and much more. All this information helps you make predictions about what you are going to read, and once you start reading, it helps you focus on the important information in the reading.

PREDICTING CONTENT USING VISUALS

PRISM Online Workbook

1 Work with a partner. You are going to read a case study about a new kind of city. Before you read, look at the photos of transportation in two cities and answer the questions.

1 What problem can you see in the first photo? Does your city have this problem?

_____

2 What is the vehicle in the second photo? How could it be a solution to the problem in Question 1? Where do you think the photo was taken?

_____

3 How are the cities in the two photos different?

_____

2 Read the definitions. Complete the sentences with the correct form of the words in bold.

> **commuter** (n) someone who travels between home and work or school regularly
> **connect** (v) to join two things or places together
> **destination** (n) the place where someone or something is going
> **outskirts** (n) the outer area of a city or town
> **public transportation** (n) a system of vehicles, such as buses and subways, which operate at regular times for public use
> **rail** (n) trains as a method of transportation
> **traffic congestion** (n) when too many vehicles use a road network and it results in slower speeds or no movement at all

1 Vancouver, British Columbia, has an outstanding system of _____ , so it isn't necessary to own a car there.
2 I like living on the _____ of the city because there is more open space and the air is cleaner.
3 I take the train to work every day because the _____ network is fast and cheap.
4 _____ has improved since my city built a subway and improved the bus system. Fewer people drive to work now.
5 I told the bus driver that my _____ was downtown, so she told me to get off on Main Street.
6 In large cities, people usually prefer to live near their workplace so that they don't have to be a _____ , but it's more expensive than the suburbs.
7 Ferries _____ the main land to the islands.

WHILE READING

3 Read the case study on page 64 and answer the questions.

1 Which features are designed to make Masdar City cooler than the area around it?

_____

2 What is a PRT, and how does it work?

_____

3 Apart from the PRT, what other transportation options are available in Masdar City?

_____

4 How did the financial crisis of 2008–2009 affect Masdar City?

_____

Masdar:
the Future of Cities?

1 Abu Dhabi, the capital of the United Arab Emirates, is a modern city with a population of about 1.5 million people. The expanding economy and rising population have brought great benefits to Abu Dhabi, but with them comes a major problem: traffic jams. Abu Dhabi, like many cities in the United Arab Emirates, suffers from **traffic congestion**, and although it is not as bad as in some cities, the average commuting time of 45 minutes is relatively high.

2 One answer to the congestion problem is Masdar City, a new city of 2.3 square miles (6 square kilometers) being built near the airport on the **outskirts** of Abu Dhabi. Masdar gets all of its electricity from solar power. There is a wall around the city to keep out the hot desert wind, and the streets are narrow. This provides shade from the sun and allows a breeze to pass through the streets. As a result, the city is about 60 °F (15 °C) cooler than Abu Dhabi.

3 There is no traffic congestion in Masdar because cars are not allowed in the city. Instead, people use **public transportation**. An underground **rail** system and a light-rail transit system run through the center of the town and **connect** Masdar to Abu Dhabi and the airport. A unique transportation system called Personal Rapid Transit (PRT) was also planned and partially built. The original plan was to have 3,000 solar-powered "podcars" that could carry passengers to about 100 stations all around the city. The vehicles would also be used to transport **commuters** from stations in the city outskirts, where they would leave their cars, to their **destinations** in the city.

4 Since 2006, Masdar City has run into serious financial difficulties. It was originally projected to cost around $24 billion, but the global financial crisis of 2008–2009 had a negative effect on the plans. In October of 2010, it was announced that the PRT would not be expanded beyond the test phase of the project. Instead, Masdar will use a fleet of electric vehicles together with the PRT and other transportation systems to move people from place to place. Meanwhile, construction continues, and Masdar City is expected to be completed sometime before 2025. When it is finished, it will have as many as 50,000 people. If all goes well, Masdar's green solutions to both traffic and environmental problems will outweigh the financial cost of building the city.

4 Read the case study again. Complete the sentences using no more than three words.

1 Abu Dhabi has a big problem with _____ .
2 The average time it takes to get to work is _____ .
3 Masdar's electricity comes from _____ .
4 Traffic jams are not a problem in Masdar because cars are _____ in the city.
5 Originally, Masdar City was supposed to cost
  $ _____ .
6 Masdar City will be completed by _____ , and _____ people will live there.

READING BETWEEN THE LINES

5 Work with a partner. Read the case study again and answer the questions.

1 What are the possible benefits of Abu Dhabi's expanding economy and rising population?

_____

_____

2 Masdar will be a small city with several advantages. What will be some disadvantages of living there?

_____

_____

3 Why do you think the planners of Masdar City decided to stop building the PRT?

_____

_____

DISCUSSION

6 Work with a partner. Discuss the questions.

1 Would you like to live in Masdar City? Why or why not?
2 Do you agree that the benefits of Masdar City will outweigh the financial cost of building it? Why or why not?
3 Would a PRT system work in your city? Why or why not?

PREPARING TO READ

1 Read the definitions. Complete the sentences with the correct form of the words in bold.

> **cycle** (v) to travel by bicycle
> **emergency** (n) an unexpected situation that requires immediate action
> **engineering** (n) the activity of designing and building things like bridges, roads, machines, etc.
> **fuel** (n) a substance like gas or coal that produces energy when it is burned
> **government** (n) the group of people that controls a country or city and makes decisions about laws, taxes, education, etc.
> **practical** (adj) useful; suitable for the situation it is being used for
> **vehicle** (n) any machine that travels on roads, such as cars, buses, etc.

1 I don't own a car, but I have a bicycle. I usually _____ to work if the weather is nice.

2 In my apartment I have a first-aid kit, a fire extinguisher, and a flashlight in case of an _____ .

3 The Danyang-Kunshan Grand Bridge in China, which is 103 miles (166 km) long, is an incredible work of _____ .

4 A Boeing 747 jet burns about 11 tons of _____ an hour in flight. That's equal to about 1 gallon (3.8 liters) each second.

5 The _____ wants people to drive less, so it passed a law that requires drivers to pay a high tax on gas.

6 In Masdar, drivers must park their _____ outside the city and use public transportation to reach the city center.

7 If I want to use public transportation, I must take three buses to get to school. This isn't _____ , so I usually drive my car.

2 Work with a partner. You are going to read an essay about solving traffic congestion. Before you read, look at the photos on page 67 and answer the questions.

1 What solutions to the problem of traffic congestion do the photographs show?

_____

2 What other solutions to traffic congestion do you think the article will discuss?

_____
_____

1   Traffic congestion is a serious problem in cities worldwide. There are simply too many **vehicles** competing for too little space. The company TomTom, which does research on traffic in cities worldwide, estimated that in 2015, the average commuter wasted 100 hours during the evening rush hour alone. In addition to wasting people's time, traffic jams have many other negative effects. Therefore, **governments** everywhere are working hard to find solutions to this problem.

2   Traffic jams have negative effects on drivers, cities, and the environment. To begin, they cause stress to drivers, which may lead to health problems or road rage[1]. Traffic jams can also lead to economic losses because products cannot be delivered on time, and employees arrive late for work or meetings. Another negative effect is that **emergency** services can become caught in traffic and are therefore unable to get to an emergency in time. Finally, traffic congestion negatively affects the environment. Traffic congestion wastes **fuel**, which in turn produces more carbon dioxide through car exhaust[2] and contributes to the greenhouse effect. Taken together, all these effects have a serious negative impact on the quality of people's lives.

3   Because of these serious effects, cities and governments everywhere are taking steps to reduce road congestion. The most obvious solutions involve **engineering**. This means building more roads with wider lanes so that more cars can travel at the same time. Also, tunnels and bridges can be constructed to guide drivers around congested areas. However, the construction costs for engineering solutions are extremely high. Another problem is that more roads may actually result in more traffic. In short, engineering solutions have both advantages and disadvantages.

4   Other, more creative, solutions to the congestion problem are to increase the tax on fuel or to make people pay to travel in the center of a city or on a freeway. If governments increase the cost of driving, people will think more carefully about using their cars. However, taxing fuel and roads may mean that some people cannot afford to drive their cars, and they may have to give up their jobs. Also, governments may not want to increase the fuel tax too much if the tax is unpopular with voters.

5   A more popular solution, therefore, would be to promote other forms of transportation, like ferries, and subways. One suggestion is to encourage people to **cycle** more. Although riding a bicycle has obvious health benefits and does not pollute the air, it is not **practical** in every climate and can prove dangerous in heavy traffic.

6   Another possibility is to persuade people to use buses, although they are inconvenient for some people. A related option is a park-and-ride system that allows people to drive to the outskirts of cities, park, and then take a bus to the city center. This allows some flexibility for car drivers and reduces congestion in the center of the city. A disadvantage for people who work late shifts[3] is that many buses do not run at night.

7   Overall, cities are using a variety of methods to tackle the problem of traffic congestion. Most of the methods have advantages as well as disadvantages. It seems that encouraging alternative forms of transportation is probably the best solution because it reduces the amount of traffic on the roads and also has a positive effect on the environment.

[1] **road rage** (n) violence committed by angry drivers in traffic
[2] **exhaust** (n) smoke that comes out of a car as a result of burning gasoline
[3] **late shifts** (n) work hours that are late in the day or at night

WHILE READING

READING FOR
MAIN IDEAS

3 Read the essay and circle the best title.

    a The Effects of Traffic Congestion in Cities
    b Solving the Problem of Traffic Congestion
    c Urban Traffic Congestion is Increasing
    d Bicycles Can Solve Urban Traffic Congestion

READING FOR DETAILS

4 Read the essay again. What are the four negative effects of traffic congestion mentioned in the essay? Write your answers.

_____ _____

_____ _____

5 Read the essay again. Complete the chart of solutions to the problem of traffic congestion. Write one word in each blank. In some items, more than one answer is possible.

	solutions	advantages	disadvantages
engineering	Build more roads, (1)_____ , and bridges.	More vehicles can (2)_____ at once.	This may (3)_____ in more traffic.
tax	Increase tax on roads and (4)_____ .	People will think more about using their cars.	Some people may need to give up their (5)_____ .
cycling	Encourage people to cycle more.	It has benefits for your (6)_____ and reduces pollution.	It can be dangerous when (7)_____ is heavy.
park-and-ride	People park and then travel into the city center by (8)_____ .	It reduces (9)_____ in the city center.	Buses may not operate at (10)_____ .

READING BETWEEN THE LINES

MAKING INFERENCES

6 Work with a partner. Answer the questions.

    1 What sort of health problems might be caused by stress?

    _____

    2 Why would a person in the government not want to have an unpopular tax?

    _____

    3 Why are buses inconvenient for some people?

    _____

DISCUSSION

7 Work with a partner. Use ideas from Reading 1 and Reading 2 to answer the following questions.

1 Are Abu Dhabi's traffic problems similar to the problems in other big cities? Give an example.

2 Review the solutions for reducing traffic congestion in Masdar City. Could these solutions work in other big cities? Why or why not?

3 In addition to the solutions suggested in Reading 1 and Reading 2, can you think of other solutions to traffic congestion?

⊙ LANGUAGE DEVELOPMENT

TRANSPORTATION COLLOCATIONS

1 Match the words to make collocations about transportation.

1	traffic	a	transportation
2	public	b	restrictions
3	bike	c	congestion
4	rush	d	lane
5	car	e	pool
6	road	f	rage
7	parking	g	hour

2 Complete the sentences with collocations from Exercise 1.

1 _____ is a big problem in this city. The traffic jams are terrible.

2 I use _____ like trains or the subway to get to work.

3 You can't drive in the _____ . It's only for bicycles.

4 Because of _____ , you can't leave your car there.

5 _____ is usually from eight to nine in the morning, and then again from four in the afternoon to seven in the evening

6 I am in a _____ and drive to work with a coworker.

7 If people get angry and behave aggressively in traffic, they are expressing _____ .

SYNONYMS FOR VERBS

3 Rewrite the sentences using the verbs from the box to replace the words in bold.

> attempt   consider   convince   prevent
> produce   reduce   require   waste

1 We **need** more public transportation in the city like a light-rail network.

_____

2 Commuters **try** to arrive on time, but traffic often causes delays.

_____

3 Masdar City is going to use solar energy to **make** all of its electricity.

_____

4 It's important for people in industrial countries to **lower** their use of energy.

_____

5 Traffic congestion causes people to **use** time and energy **in an inefficient way**.

_____

6 We should **think about** cycling instead of using our cars to travel short distances.

_____

7 New roads will **stop** traffic congestion in the short term.

_____

8 It will be difficult to **get** drivers to use public transportation.

_____

WRITING

CRITICAL THINKING

At the end of this unit, you will write two paragraphs about possible solutions to a problem. Look at this unit's Writing Task below.

▶ Discuss the advantages and disadvantages of two solutions to a city's traffic congestion problems.

1 Work with a partner. Look back at Reading 2. Complete the chart with information from Reading 2.

Problem	Goal(s)

Solutions	Advantages/Disadvantages	
	+	
	−	
	+	
	−	
	+	
	−	
	+	
	−	

Decisions(s)	Reason(s)

2 Study the map. List the city's potential traffic problems.

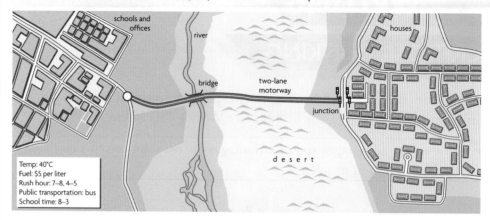

The residential area is on one side of the bridge, and the business center and schools are on the other side.

3 Complete the chart with the main problem and goals for solving the problem.

Problem	Goal(s)

Solutions	Advantages/Disadvantages
	+
	−
	+
	−
	+
	−
	+
	−

Decisions(s)	Reason(s)

4 Look at the map again and the possible solutions to the traffic problem. What are the advantages of each problem? What are the disadvantages? Choose four solutions and write their advantages and disadvantages in the chart on the opposite page.

build a tunnel	encourage people to cycle
Cost: $3 million	Cost: $500,000
Time to implement: 2 years	Time to implement: 3 months
park-and-ride bus system	**move the residential area to the other side of the river**
Cost: $2 million	Cost: $100 million
Time to implement: 1 year	Time to implement: 10 years
road tax	**ferry**
Cost: $100,000	$2.5 million
Time to implement: 3 months	Time to implement: 2 years

5 Look at the four solutions and choose the best two. Write them in the Decision(s) box and write your reasons in the Reason(s) box on the opposite page.

GRAMMAR FOR WRITING

FUTURE REAL CONDITIONAL

LANGUAGE

You can use future real conditionals to persuade or negotiate. Notice the use of *if* and *will* to combine two sentences.

idea/action: The government increases tax on fuel.

consequence: People use their cars less.

If the government increases the tax on fuel, people **will** use their cars less.
or
People **will** use their cars less **if** the government increases the tax on fuel.

Notice:

- The idea/action clause begins with *if*.
- The consequence clause uses *will*.
- *Can* changes to *be able to* in the consequence clause.
- Either the idea clause or the consequence clause can come first. If the idea clause comes first, put a comma after it.

1 Join the pairs of sentences using *if* and *will*. Remember to change *can* in Question 5. More than one answer is possible.

1 We move the offices and schools next to the houses. We have fewer traffic problems.

_____

2 We have a ferry over the river. Fewer people use the bridge.

_____

3 Fewer cars use the roads. We increase the price of fuel.

_____

4 We change the office hours. The cars won't all use the road at the same time.

_____

5 We build a railway line. People can use the train instead of their cars.

_____

IF ... NOT AND UNLESS

You can also use *if ... not* or *unless* to describe the consequence of not doing a certain action.

idea/action: The government increases tax on fuel.
consequence: People use their cars less.

If the government **doesn't** increase tax on fuel, people **won't** use their cars less.
Unless the government increases tax on fuel, people **won't** use their cars less.

2 Join the sentences using *if ... not* or *unless*.

1 The traffic will improve. We build more roads.
    The traffic will not improve if we don't build more roads.

2 Pollution will be reduced. We use cleaner transportation.

_____

3 We provide a solution. People will get to work on time.

_____

4 We will solve the traffic problem. We build houses closer to the business areas.

_____

5 The city invests in a PRT. There will be less congestion.

_____

ACADEMIC WRITING SKILLS

WRITING A CONCLUDING SENTENCE

Some paragraphs have a concluding sentence. Usually, this sentence reminds the reader of the topic sentence. It can do this by restating the main idea, but with different words. It can also summarize the main points of the paragraph. Writers often add a concluding comment, such as their opinion or a prediction. Compare these topic sentences and concluding sentences:

Topic sentence: Since 2006, Masdar City has run into serious financial difficulties.

Concluding sentence: If all goes well, Masdar's green solutions to both traffic and environmental problems will outweigh the financial cost of building the city.

1 Read the paragraphs. Circle the best concluding sentence for each one.

Paragraph 1

Riding my bicycle to school has both advantages and disadvantages. The most important advantage is that it saves me time because I don't have to wait in traffic or spend time searching for a parking space. Cycling is great exercise, and it feels good. Also, cycling helps the environment because it does not create any pollution. However, there are two things I dislike about cycling. One is that it can be dangerous if drivers can't see you. Also, some drivers are very rude.

---

a In other words, some drivers think they own the road and cyclists have no place on it.
b Still, I think the advantages of cycling outweigh the disadvantages, and I will continue to use my bicycle to get around in good weather.
c Because of these disadvantages, I may sell my bike and take the bus.

Paragraph 2

In some cities, such as Seattle and Istanbul, people commute to work by ferry. A ferry carries people, and sometimes cars, over water between two or more places. Sometimes a ferry is the only way to get around because there are no roads or bridges. However, even if a road exists, many people prefer to travel by ferry because it saves time. Ferry passengers don't have to sit in traffic, and they can read or work on their computers. Another benefit is that ferries help the environment by keeping hundreds of cars and trucks off the roads.

---

a These advantages explain why people in cities all over the world travel to and from work by ferry.
b For me, the best thing about taking the ferry to work is that it is fun.
c Many ferries have a restaurant on board, and passengers can drink coffee or eat a meal while they commute.

Discuss the advantages and disadvantages of two solutions to a city's traffic congestion problems.

PLAN

1 Look at the chart you created in Exercise 3 in Critical Thinking and complete the outline.

Solution 1: _____

Advantages: _____

_____

Disadvantages: _____

_____

Solution 2: _____

Advantages: _____

_____

Disadvantages: _____

_____

2 Review the Task Checklist on page 77 as you prepare your paragraphs.

WRITE A FIRST DRAFT

3 Read the introduction and conclusion to the essay and complete the essay by writing about the advantages and disadvantages of two solutions to Riverton's traffic problems. Write a concluding sentence for each paragraph.

Solving Riverton's Traffic Congestion Problem

Introduction: Riverton's unusual geography causes it to have bad traffic congestion. People have to travel from their homes on one side of the river to their offices and schools on the other. Unfortunately, there is only one main road running through the city center and just one bridge that connects the residential and business areas. Moreover, the only public transportation is a bus that uses the same road. There is also a junction near the housing area where the traffic builds up during the two rush hours, when people commute to work or drop off their children at school. After a long period of study, we have proposed two possible solutions to the traffic problems in Riverton. Both solutions have advantages and disadvantages.

Conclusion: In conclusion, of the many solutions that we have considered, these two had the most advantages. Although these plans are not perfect, there is no doubt that they will help reduce the traffic congestion in Riverton. This will have benefits both for people's health and for the environment. The people of Riverton should support these solutions.

REVISE

4 Use the Task Checklist to review your essay for content and structure. If you have any problems with content, look back at the Critical Thinking section.

TASK CHECKLIST	✔
Did you write two solution paragraphs in the main body? Do the topic sentences state the solutions?	
Did you explain the advantages and disadvantages of each solution?	
Did you write a concluding sentence for each paragraph?	

5 Make any necessary changes to your essay.

EDIT

6 Use the Language Checklist to edit your essay for language errors.

LANGUAGE CHECKLIST	✔
Did you use transportation collocations correctly?	
Did you use synonyms for verbs to make your writing more interesting and academic?	
Did you use future real conditionals correctly?	
Did you use *if, will, unless* and *if ... not* correctly?	

7 Make any necessary changes to your essay.

CREATING IDEA MAPS

SKILLS

Students have to do a lot of reading at college and university. There is also a lot to remember. Idea maps are one way to help you organize and remember the ideas in a textbook. They are also called concept, chapter, or mind maps. Search online for examples of different kinds of idea maps.

PREPARING TO READ

1 You are going to read a handout from an architecture class. Before you read, work with a partner and discuss the questions.

    1 When you read a textbook, how do you organize and remember the information?

    2 What kinds of notes do you write while you are reading a textbook?

ARCHITECTURE 302 Urban Environments

Teaching Assistant: Tina Stevens

There are many ways to organize the information you learn from a reading. One way to do that is to create an idea map. Students make idea maps for several reasons:

- They can understand how everything is connected.
- It is easier to remember information that is organized as a map.
- It is easier to find the information they need later.

In an idea map, there is a lot of information on one page. When you create a map, use only words or short phrases, not whole sentences.

Here are the steps for making an idea map:

- Start with the main topic in the center of the page.
- Connect the important related ideas to the main topic.
- Then, include details for each important related idea.
- Add lines to show connections between things.
- Add your own ideas from experience or knowledge about the topic.

Here are some suggestions to make your map easier to read:

- Use different colors for different branches.
- Draw simple pictures or symbols.

Here is an example of an idea map from the article about Masdar City on page 64.

I hope this helps you. It is something you can use in all of your classes. Let me know if you have questions.

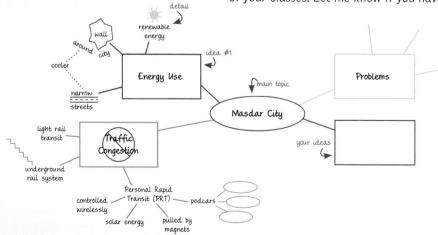

WHILE READING

2 Read the handout and circle the correct option to complete the sentences.

1 Idea maps help students _____ .
   a see the relationships between things
   b be more creative

2 Organizing information into an idea map makes the information easier to _____ .
   a understand
   b remember

3 In idea maps, the writer should use _____ .
   a whole sentences
   b a word or short phrase

4 A idea map might be easier to read with _____ .
   a color and pictures
   b more detail

3 Read the handout again and answer the questions.

1 What is the main topic of the map? _____

2 How many important related ideas are on the map? _____

3 How many details about energy use are on the map?

   _____

4 What does the sun represent on the map? _____

PRACTICE

4 Work with a partner. Copy the unfinished idea map in the reading and do the following.

1 Add three details about the podcars.

2 Add three examples of problems with Masdar City.

3 Add your own ideas about Masdar City: what would work, what wouldn't work, your opinion about Masdar City, etc.

REAL-WORLD APPLICATION

5 Work with a partner. Read the article about traffic congestion on page 67 again and create an idea map.

a Use a blank piece of paper.

b Start with the word Traffic Congestion as the main topic in the center.

c Add the important ideas.

d Add details.

e Add your idea from your experience or knowledge.

6 Share your map with your class.

LEARNING OBJECTIVES

Reading skill	Annotate
Grammar	Paraphrase
Academic writing skill	Write a summary and a personal response
Writing Task	Write a summary paragraph and personal response
On Campus	Communicate with professors

CUSTOMS AND TRADITIONS

ACTIVATE YOUR KNOWLEDGE

Work with a partner. Discuss the questions.

1 Which celebration is shown in the photo? Are the customs and traditions at this event the same in your country?

2 What traditional celebrations do you have in your culture?

3 Which countries have you visited? What surprised you about the customs or traditions of the places you visited?

PREPARING TO WATCH

1 You are going to watch a video about Halloween. Before you watch, work with a partner and discuss the questions.

1 When do people wear traditional clothes in your country? When do they wear costumes? Why?

2 Do people ever decorate their homes for special events? How?

3 Do people ever eat special foods to celebrate events and holidays? Which ones?

2 Work with a partner. Look at the photos from the video and discuss the questions.

1 What do people do on Halloween?

2 What does "1 billion pounds" refer to?

3 What is the girl looking at in the store?

GLOSSARY

purchase (v) to buy

Halloween (n) a holiday on October 31st when children wear costumes, visit other houses, and say "trick or treat" to ask for candy

costume (n) a set of clothes that someone wears to make them look like someone or something else, e.g., in a play

pumpkin (n) a large, round vegetable with thick, orange skin

Celtic (adj) related to the ancient people of Ireland, Scotland, and Wales

retailer (n) a person or business that sells products to the public

---

WHILE WATCHING

3 ▶ Watch the video. Circle the correct answer.

1 On Halloween people eat a lot of *candy / pumpkins*.
2 Many people wear *scarves / costumes* on Halloween.
3 Halloween is based on an old Celtic *religion / tradition*.
4 Retailers think Halloween is *good / not good* for business.
5 The average *person / retailer* spends about $75 on Halloween.

4 ▶ Watch the video again. Write *T* (true), *F* (false), or *DNS* (does not say) next to the statements. Then, correct the false statements.

_____ 1 Tens of billions of trick-or-treaters celebrate Halloween.

_____

_____ 2 The most expensive variety of candy is chocolate.

_____

_____ 3 Illinois produces the most Halloween costumes.

_____

_____ 4 U.S. retailers make more money on Christmas than Halloween.

_____

_____ 5 Halloween is celebrated in many countries.

_____

5 Work with a partner and discuss the questions. Give reasons for your answers.

1 Is Halloween more popular with children or adults? Why?
2 Why do people dress in costumes on Halloween?
3 During which holiday in the United States do people spend the most money?

DISCUSSION

6 Work in a small group. Discuss the questions.

1 Have you ever worn a costume for Halloween or for another special occasion? Describe it.
2 Do people in your country celebrate Halloween? Why or why not?
3 Why might some Americans not want to celebrate Halloween?

READING

READING 1

UNDERSTANDING
KEY VOCABULARY

PREPARING TO READ

1 You are going to read an article about customs and traditions in different countries. Before you read the article, read the definitions below. Complete the sentences with the correct form of the words in bold.

> **appearance** (n) the way someone or something looks
> **culture** (n) a society with its own ideas, traditions, and ways of behaving
> **exchange** (v) to give something to someone, and receive something that they give you
> **expect** (v) to think that something will or should happen
> **formal** (adj) correct or conservative in style, dress, or speech; not casual
> **greet** (v) to welcome someone with particular words or actions
> **relationship** (n) the way two people or groups feel and behave toward each other

1 I love traveling because I enjoy experiencing other _____ and their food, celebrations, and traditions.
2 In many traditional wedding ceremonies, it's usual for the bride and groom to _____ rings.
3 In Korea and some Spanish-speaking countries, people do not _____ a woman to change her last name when she gets married.
4 In Thailand, people _____ each other by holding their hands together, bowing, and saying "Sawadee," which is similar to "Hello" or "Good day" in English.
5 Many languages have two ways to say *you*. They have a _____ word to use in polite situations like work and a different word for family and friends.
6 On their wedding day, most brides spend a lot of time and effort on their _____ . They want every detail of their hair, clothes, and makeup to be perfect.
7 In most cultures, people who have a close _____ enjoy spending time together and giving each other gifts.

2 What "rules" do visitors to your country need to know in order to be polite? Write notes in the chart.

custom / behavior	rules
greeting (kissing, shaking hands, etc.)	
giving gifts	
behavior in business meetings	
business dress code	
punctuality	

3 Work in a small group. Discuss the following questions.

1 Share the information from your charts. Which "rules" from your charts are similar? Which are different?
2 The article discusses correct behavior in Brazil, Japan, and India. What do you know about the unique customs of these countries?

WHILE READING

 SKILLS

Annotating

Active readers annotate while reading. Use a system that you find easy to use and understand. Below are some suggestions:

- Highlight the main ideas in a bright color or put brackets ([ ]) around them.
- Highlight key words and phrases in a different color. Use colors consistently.
- Underline, circle, or box important details such as examples, reasons, and supporting arguments. In the margin, identify the type of detail you marked.

Also, as you read, write notes in the margins: summarize main ideas in your own words, outline or list important supporting details, write any questions you have, write your opinion or your reaction to the text. Interacting with the text in this way will help you learn and remember the important information.

4 Read the article on customs around the world. Annotate the text while you read. Part of the text has been annotated as an example.

5 Read the article again. Circle the customs that are not mentioned in the article.

a greetings
b personal space
c giving gifts
d business meetings

e table manners
f giving business cards
g being punctual

CUSTOMS AROUND THE WORLD
BY ANDY SCHMIDT

1 In recent decades foreign travel has become a multi-billion dollar industry. International travel has many benefits, but tourists can run into trouble if they don't take the time to learn about the **cultures** they're visiting. It is very important for travelers to take the time to learn about the cultures they are visiting so that they know what to **expect** and how to avoid cultural misunderstandings. That is why we are presenting this "Customs Around the World" series, where we will look at three different cultures every month to help you become a well-informed traveler. This month's exciting destinations are Brazil, Japan, and India.

Why learn about cultures before travel—
- *know what to expect*
- *avoid misunderstandings*

BRAZIL

2 In general, Brazilian culture is informal. Most Brazilians are very friendly people, so it is important to say hello and goodbye to everyone. Women kiss men and each other on the cheek, but men usually just shake hands. Brazilians typically stand very close to each other and touch each other's arms, elbows, and back regularly while speaking. You should not move away if this happens. If you go to a business meeting, you are not expected to take a gift. In fact, an expensive gift can be seen as suspicious[1].

Brazil— friendly, informal; greetings important

3 On the other hand, if you are invited to someone's house, you should take a gift—for example, flowers or chocolate. However, stay clear of anything purple or black, as these colors are related to death.

4 If you are invited to dinner, arrive at least 30 minutes late, but always dress well because a person's **appearance** is very important to Brazilians.

JAPAN

5 The Japanese are quite different from the Brazilians. They can be quite **formal**, so don't stand too close. Kissing or touching other people in public is not common. When you meet Japanese people, they may shake your hand, although bowing is the more traditional greeting.

6 In a business meeting, the Japanese often like to know what your position is in your company before they talk to you. You should hand over a business card using both hands, and when you receive a business card, you should immediately read it carefully. It is important to be punctual[2] in Japan. You should arrive early and dress formally. Gifts are often **exchanged**, but the recipient may refuse the gift at least once before accepting it. You should remember to do the same if you receive a gift. When you present your gift, you should say that it is just a token of your appreciation[3].

INDIA

7 India is a huge country with many languages, cultures, and religions. Customs differ from region to region. However, in general, you should know that hierarchy[4] is important in India. Therefore, when you meet Indians, it is important to **greet** the oldest or the most senior person first. Men may shake hands with men, and women often also shake hands with women, but men and women tend not to shake hands.

8 Personal **relationships** are important in business in India, and you should not be surprised if the first meeting is spent getting to know everyone. In addition, it is important to know that many Indians do not like to say "no," so it may be difficult to know what they are really thinking. Appointments are necessary and punctuality is important. Business dress is formal, so men and women should wear dark suits.

9 If you are invited to an Indian's home, arrive on time. You do not have to bring a gift, but gifts are not refused. However, do not bring white flowers because these are used in funerals[5].

[1]**suspicious** (adj) causing a feeling of distrust or that something is wrong
[2]**punctual** (adj) on time
[3]**token of your appreciation** (n) an inexpensive gift meant to express thanks or gratitude
[4]**hierarchy** (n) status; a system for organizing people according to their importance
[5]**funeral** (n) the ceremony held after someone has died

6 Complete the student's notes with words and phrases from the article.

custom/behavior	Brazil	Japan	India
greeting	Women (1)_____ other women & men. Men (2)_____ other men.	OK to (3)_____ , but (4)_____ is more traditional.	Greet (5)_____ person first. Women shake hands with (6)_____ , men with (7)_____ .
gifts	Bring a gift to someone's (8)_____ .	Receiving: Common to (9)_____ before you accept. Giving: Say it is just a (10)_____ .	Not (11)_____ , but do not bring (12)_____ .
business behavior	Do not bring a (13)_____ .	Hand over your business card with (14)_____ . When you receive a business card, (15)_____ .	• (16)_____ meeting spent getting to know everyone. • Many Indians do not like to say (17)_____ . • (18)_____ are necessary.
dress/appearance	Dress (19)_____ .	Dress (20)_____ .	Business dress is (21)_____ .
punctuality	Arrive (22)_____ .	Arrive (23)_____ .	Arrive (24)_____ .

READING BETWEEN THE LINES

7 Work with a partner. Answer the questions.

1 In Brazil, why would people probably be suspicious of an expensive gift?

_____

2 Why shouldn't you move away if Brazilians touch you during conversation?

_____

3 Why would Japanese businesspeople want to know your position in a company?

_____

4 What could be the reason why Indians don't like to say "no"?

_____

5 What can be the negative result of a cultural misunderstanding?

_____

DISCUSSION

8 Work with a partner. Discuss the questions.

1 What new information did you learn about Brazil, Japan, and India from reading the article?

2 Which of these countries would you like to visit? Why?

3 Have you ever gotten into trouble in a foreign country because you didn't know the customs or rules of the culture? What was your mistake?

READING 2

PREPARING TO READ

1 You are going to read an article about nontraditional weddings. Before you read the article, read the definitions below. Complete the sentences with the correct form of the words in bold.

> **belief** (n) an idea that you are certain is true
> **ceremony** (n) a formal event with special traditions, activities, or words, such as a wedding
> **couple** (n) two people who are married or in a relationship
> **engaged** (adj) having a formal agreement to get married
> **reception** (n) a formal party that is given to celebrate a special event or to welcome someone
> **relative** (n) any member of your family
> **theme** (n) the main idea, subject, or topic of an event, book, musical piece, etc.

1 In Mexican culture, a *quinceñera* is a special __ _____ to celebrate a girl's fifteenth birthday.

2 A honeymoon is a time for a newly married _____ to relax after the wedding and spend time alone.

3 Children tend to have the same _____ as their parents when they are young, but this may change when they become adults.

4 My sister and her boyfriend became _____ on New Year's Eve, and their wedding will be after they both graduate from college.

5 My sister loves 80s music, so we're having an 80s _____ for her birthday celebration.

6 My cousin's wedding took place in city hall, and the _____ afterwards was held in a hotel.

7 I have a large family with many aunts, uncles, and cousins. It's fun to get together with all my _____ on special occasions.

Nontraditional Weddings
by Serena Lessler

1   Even if they have never attended a traditional American wedding in person, most people have probably seen such weddings in movies or on television. The beautiful bride in her white dress, the handsome groom, the **ceremony** in the church, the romantic music—these customs are familiar to people all over the world. Though most American **couples** still choose to have this kind of traditional wedding, more and more couples these days are planning unique weddings that reflect their **beliefs**, hobbies, and personal style. Three types of nontraditional weddings are adventure weddings, destination weddings, and **theme** weddings.

2   Adventure weddings typically combine the marriage ceremony with a physical activity that has special meaning for the couple. Cathy and Frank Mason, enthusiastic scuba divers who had participated in dives all over the world, met on a shark-diving adventure near Key West, Florida, in 2012. A year later they were **engaged** and were starting to plan their wedding. Cathy had always dreamed of a large, traditional wedding in a church, but from the start Frank had a different idea. Why not have a wedding that combined their love for each other and the activity they loved most—scuba diving? Cathy finally agreed, and the couple were married underwater in May, 2015—surrounded by numerous friends and **relatives,** all in scuba gear. Other adventure-seeking couples have been known to get married while surfing, skydiving, or riding in a hot-air balloon.

3   Most people are less adventurous than the Masons, but many of them love to travel. It is becoming more and more common for such couples to get married in a distant location. An American couple, Arielle Cogan and Richard Thompson, met when both of them were spending a year studying history in Edinburgh, Scotland. After they became engaged, they discovered that neither of them was interested in an ordinary wedding. Instead, they were married in a small, 18th-century church in Edinburgh with just their families and a few close friends as guests. The bride wore a traditional white dress and the groom wore a kilt, which is a traditional Scottish skirt for men! Destination weddings allow couples to get married in the place of their dreams. The main disadvantage is the cost: It can be expensive to have family and friends fly to an exotic location on the other side of the world.

4   A theme wedding allows couples to create a fun, nontraditional wedding that centers around a beloved book, song, story, or historical period. A couple from Epping, New Hampshire, planned every detail of their wedding, from the wedding vows to the food at the **reception**, around the theme of the *Harry Potter* books by J.K. Rowling. Other unique themes for weddings have included pirates, superheroes like Superman, a Hawaiian luau, country music, Victorian England, the 1960s, a fairy tale like "Cinderella", and many, many more.

5   Unlike the past, when a traditional religious wedding was the only option available to marrying couples, couples these days are free to choose almost any type of wedding they can imagine. The variety of wedding styles and locations is perhaps a reflection of the general trend toward individual choice and self expression that has been growing stronger in the U.S. since the 1960s. But whether a couple chooses an old-fashioned church wedding or a ceremony at the top of a mountain, the central purpose of a wedding—to celebrate the union of a couple in the presence of the people who love them—has not changed, and it probably never will.

2 Work with a partner. Look at the title and the photos on page 89 and answer the questions.

1 What is happening in the photos? Where do you think they were taken?

_____

2 Is this type of thing becoming more popular in your country or culture?

_____

3 How would your family react if you decided to have a wedding like the couples in the photos?

_____

_____

WHILE READING

3 Read the article and annotate the text. Look at page 85 for what to annotate.

4 Use your notes and annotations for Reading 2 to put the following main ideas in the order they were discussed in the article.

theme weddings _____
adventure weddings _____
reasons for the popularity of nontraditional weddings _____
destination weddings _____
choices for couples who want a nontraditional wedding _____

5 Circle the best summary.

a The text describes a traditional American wedding and gives examples of nontraditional weddings.
b The text contrasts traditional and modern relationships in the United States.
c The text describes marriage customs around the world.
d The text describes a religious wedding in the United States.

6 Correct the factual mistakes in the sentences.

1 In a traditional wedding, the bride wears a white suit.

_____

2 Frank Mason wanted a traditional wedding in a church.

_____

3 Destination weddings take place close to the bride and groom's home.

_____

4 Getting married underwater is a kind of theme wedding.

_____

5 The couple from Epping, New Hampshire, had an adventure wedding.

_____

6 Today there are few options for couples who want a nontraditional wedding.

_____

READING BETWEEN THE LINES

7 Work with a partner. Answer the questions.

MAKING INFERENCES

1 These days, do most American couples choose to have traditional or nontraditional weddings? Why?

_____

2 What might be the disadvantages of an adventure wedding or a theme wedding?

_____

3 What kind of people might choose to have each type of wedding described in the article?

_____

DISCUSSION

8 Work with a partner. Use ideas from Reading 1 and Reading 2 to answer the following questions.

SYNTHESIZING

1 Imagine that you are going to attend a wedding in Brazil, Japan, or India. How will you dress? What time should you arrive? What type of gift should you give? What type of gift would you avoid giving?

2 If you could have one of the nontraditional weddings described in the reading, which type would you choose? Why?

3 Why do you think more American couples are choosing to have nontraditional weddings these days? Is this true in your country as well?

4 Besides weddings, are any other traditional celebrations in your country changing? How?

AVOIDING GENERALIZATIONS

In academic English, be careful not to make general statements unless you have the data to prove them. A reader of the example sentence below can argue that not all weddings are expensive.

Weddings are expensive.

You can avoid generalizations by using words such as *many, can,* or *tend to.*

Quantifier
Many weddings are expensive.

Verb
Weddings **tend to be** expensive.

Modal verb
Weddings **can be** expensive.

PRISM Online Workbook

1 Read the generalizations. Use the words in parentheses to make the sentences more accurate.

1 We tip the waiter in restaurants. (tend to)

_____

2 Formal weddings are less common these days. (tend to)

_____

3 Anniversaries are important. (can)

_____

4 Common hand gestures like waving are misunderstood in a different culture. (can)

_____

5 In Mexico, old people live with their children. (most)

_____

ADVERBS OF FREQUENCY TO AVOID GENERALIZATIONS

You can also use adverbs of frequency to avoid generalizations. They are:

⟶

0%					100%
never	seldom	occasionally	often	usually	always
	hardly ever	sometimes		almost always	
	rarely			normally	

Notice the position of the adverbs in the sentences.

Before the main verb

People **usually** have barbecues in summer.

After the verb *to be*

Weddings are **often** difficult to organize.

2 Read the generalizations. Use the adverbs in parentheses to make the sentences more accurate.

PRISM Online Workbook

1 In the past, the bride's family paid for the wedding. (usually)

    _____

2 Outdoor weddings are cheaper than church weddings. (often)

    _____

3 Professionals get upset if you don't use their correct title. (sometimes)

    _____

4 Cultural knowledge is helpful in business situations. (frequently)

    _____

5 In Japan, you should arrive on time for an appointment. (always)

    _____

SYNONYMS TO AVOID REPETITION

3 Replace the words in bold in the sentences with the synonyms in the box.

PRISM Online Workbook

brief   certain   common   important   obvious   separate   serious

1 The wedding was **short**, and we went straight to the reception.

    _____

2 The high cost of weddings is a **bad** problem for many families. _____

3 The bride and groom live in **different** houses until after the wedding.

    _____

4 In **some** countries, marriage is becoming less popular. _____

5 In the past, people often married into **powerful** families for money and status. _____

6 Some customs and traditions are not **clear** to people who are visiting a country for the first time. _____

7 It is **usual** for people in my country to have large families. _____

WRITING

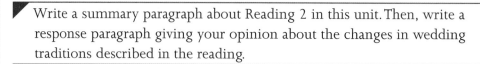

CRITICAL THINKING

At the end of this unit, you will write a summary paragraph and a response paragraph about Reading 2. Look at this unit's Writing Task below.

> Write a summary paragraph about Reading 2 in this unit. Then, write a response paragraph giving your opinion about the changes in wedding traditions described in the reading.

▲ ANALYZE

1 Look back at Reading 2 on page 89. Then, answer the questions by writing notes in the chart below.

   1 What was the main idea of the reading? Write a short sentence in the chart.

   2 Look at each paragraph of Reading 2. What was the topic? Which example(s) did the author give? Which advantages and disadvantages did the writer include? Write these details in the chart.

   3 What was the author's conclusion? Write it in your own words. (Hint: The main idea and conclusion should be similar.)

	text	my response
Reading 2		
paragraph 1 main idea		
paragraph 2	<u>Topic</u>: adventure wedding <u>Example</u>: couple got married underwater <u>Advantage</u>: combine their love of scuba diving with their love for each other	
paragraph 3		
paragraph 4		
conclusion		

Responding to an author's ideas

When responding to a text you have read, you should address each of the author's main ideas with your own point of view. How you respond will depend on how you feel about each point. Some common ways people respond to an author's ideas are:

- Agreeing or disagreeing with the author's points or ideas
- Giving an example from your own experience or of someone you know
- Connecting the author's ideas to something you read or heard from another source
- Describing how an idea makes you feel or what it reminds you of
- Evaluating the point or idea. For example, saying whether you think that it is positive or negative

2 Write your responses to each part of Reading 2 in the chart on the opposite page. Use the points in the skill box as a guide.

EVALUATE ▲

GRAMMAR FOR WRITING

PARAPHRASING

Paraphrasing means rewriting someone else's ideas in your own words. This skill is important, especially in college, because copying another person's exact words is considered to be a kind of stealing.

To paraphrase, begin by reading the original text. For example:

International travel has many benefits, but tourists can run into trouble if they don't take the time to learn about the cultures they are visiting. (Andy Schmidt, Tourism magazine)

Some strategies for paraphrasing are.

Replace words or phrases with synonyms.	Foreign travel has many advantages, but travelers can have problems unless they spend time learning the customs of the places they are visiting.
Change the order of some words or phrases.	Foreign travel has many advantages, but unless travelers learn about the customs of the places they are visiting, they can have problems.
Use indirect speech. *According to X, ...* X *states / writes / believes (that)* ...* X *says (that) ...*	**According to** Andy Schmidt in *Tourism* magazine, foreign travel has many advantages, but ... Andy Schmidt in *Tourism* magazine **states that** foreign travel has many advantages, but ...

* *That* is often left out in this type of sentence.

1 Read the original sentence and three paraphrases. Match the paraphrase with the strategy the writer used.

Original text: Brazilians typically stand very close to each other and touch each other's arms, elbows, and back regularly while speaking. (Andy Schmidt, *Tourism* magazine)

1 According to Andy Schmidt, Brazilians tend to stand very close to each other and touch each other's arms, elbows, and back regularly while speaking.

2 Brazilian people tend to stand quite close to one another, and they frequently touch each other on the upper body while they are talking.

3 While they are talking, Brazilian people tend to stand very close to one another and touch each other's backs, arms, or elbows frequently.

a use synonyms
b change the order of words or phrases
c use indirect speech

2 Paraphrase the sentences from Reading 2 using the strategy in parentheses.

1 Though most American couples still choose to have this kind of traditional wedding, more and more couples these days are planning unique weddings that reflect their beliefs, hobbies, and personal style. (use synonyms)

_____

_____

_____

2 Cathy had always dreamed of a large, traditional wedding in a church, but from the start Frank had a different idea. (use synonyms and change the order of words or phrases)

_____

_____

_____

3 Other unique themes for weddings have included pirates, superheroes such as Superman, a Hawaiian luau, country music, Victorian England, the 1960s, a fairy tale like "Cinderella", and many, many more. (Source: Serena Lessler) (use all three techniques)

_____

_____

_____

ACADEMIC WRITING SKILLS

WRITING A SUMMARY AND A PERSONAL RESPONSE

Writing a summary and a personal response is an opportunity to evaluate and express opinions about a writer's ideas.

A **summary** is a short paragraph that states the main ideas and important points of a longer text. You should always write a summary in your own words, but be sure not to change the original author's ideas. The paragraph should not include your opinion.

In a **response** paragraph you should give your ideas about the points in the summary. Your response can include examples from your personal experience, facts, or knowledge from other sources. Language that you can use includes the following:

I agree/disagree with the author that ... because ...   I think that ...
In my opinion, ...   In my experience, ...

PRISM Online Workbook

1 Read Reading 1 on page 86 again. Then, read a student's summary and response below. Answer the questions that follow on page 98.

Summary and Response

In the article "Customs Around the World," author Andy Schmidt says it is important for tourists to learn about the customs of other countries in order to prevent cultural misunderstandings in the places they are visiting. Schmidt focuses on three countries—Brazil, Japan, and India—and describes some customs visitors should know about. According to the author, Brazilians are informal people. They touch a lot, and punctuality is not always expected on some occasions. Japanese culture is exactly the opposite. People don't touch in public, and there are rules for how to exchange business cards, how to dress, what kind of gifts to give, and when to arrive at a meeting or someone's home. Indian culture is also formal, and some of the rules are similar to those in Japan. For example, it's important to arrive on time for business meetings. The author stresses the importance of personal relationships and cautions that Indian people avoid saying "no" if possible.

I definitely agree with the author's main point: It is easy to make a mistake if you don't know about other people's customs. To give an example from my own experience, I was traveling in India when I was invited to a wedding there. I had never been to an Indian wedding, so I decided to do some reading about it. One of the things I learned is that a guest should never wear white to an Indian wedding because white is associated with death. In short, these examples remind us that travelers, including me, must study the customs of a new country before visiting it.

1 Which sentence restates the main idea in Reading 1, page 86?

_____

2 Compare the main idea sentence in Reading 1 and the main idea sentence of the summary paragraph. Which paraphrasing strategies from the box on page 95 did the summary writer use?

_____

3 What other information from Reading 1 did the writer include in the summary paragraph?

_____

4 Which examples from Reading 1 did the writer include in the summary? Do you think this is too much, too little, or the right amount of detail?

_____

5 How many references to the author are there in the summary paragraph? Underline them.

6 Where does the writer give her opinion? Underline the sentence.

7 How does the writer support her opinion?

_____

8 How does the writer conclude the essay? What transition does she use?

_____

WRITING TASK

PRISM Online Workbook

Write a summary paragraph about Reading 2 in this unit. Then, write a response paragraph giving your opinion about the changes in wedding traditions described in the reading.

PLAN

1 Look at the chart you created in Exercises 1 and 2 in Critical Thinking. Then, complete an outline for your summary and response paragraphs, using the following structure.

Summary paragraph
topic sentence (author's main idea)
supporting detail 1
supporting detail 2
supporting detail 3

> **Response Paragraph**
> topic sentence (my reaction to the author's main idea)
> supporting detail 1
> supporting detail 2
> supporting detail 3 (optional)
> concluding sentence (restates your opinion)

2 Review the Task Checklist below as you prepare your paragraphs.

WRITE A FIRST DRAFT

3 Write your summary paragraph and personal response paragraph.

REVISE

4 Use the Task Checklist to review your paragraphs for content and structure.

TASK CHECKLIST	✔
Did you restate the author's main idea in your own words?	
Did you summarize the details for each type of wedding?	
Did you give examples or other supporting details for your opinion in the response paragraph?	
Did you restate your opinion in the concluding sentence?	

5 Make any necessary changes to your paragraphs.

EDIT

6 Use the Language Checklist to edit your essay/paragraph for language errors.

LANGUAGE CHECKLIST	✔
Did you use quantifiers, verbs and modals to avoid generalizations?	
Did you use adverbs of frequency correctly?	
Did you replace adjectives with synonyms to avoid repetition?	
Did you use paraphrasing to rewrite someone else's ideas?	

7 Make any necessary changes to your paragraphs.

COMMUNICATING WITH PROFESSORS

During their time at college, students need to communicate with their professors on a regular basis. The relationship that professors have with their students is different from a high-school teacher's relationship with their students, and it is important that students communicate with professors in the right way so that they have a positive and respectful relationship with them.

PREPARING TO READ

1 You are going to read an email exchange between a student and her professor. Before you read, work with a partner and discuss the questions.

1 Have you ever communicated with a professor or instructor outside of class? If so, how did you do it?

2 What are some reasons a student might contact a professor?

3 In your opinion, what is the best way to contact a professor outside of class?

On Feb.12, David Alcott wrote:
To: Sunbaby123@mail.cup.com
Re: Hi

Dear Linda,
Please come see me tomorrow during my office hours.
Sincerely,
Professor Alcott

On Feb 11, Linda Sun wrote:

hey dave—I had to miss the last few classes because of my work schedule. did i miss something important? can u send me the handouts and your presentation slides? i haven't been able to buy the book yet :(but i will get notes from someone else in the class.

Thanks!

WHILE READING

2 Work with a partner. Read the email exchange on page 100 and answer the questions that follow with a partner.

1 Why do you think Professor Alcott wants to see Linda?

_____

2 What is the tone of the professor's response? Is it the same as Linda's?

_____

3 Check all of the things that Linda did not do in her email.

a apologize ☐

b sign her message ☐

c use correct spelling
and punctuation ☐

d include the date
in her message ☐

e use the professor's last name ☐

f include a useful subject line ☐

g offer to make up for
her mistakes ☐

h use her college email
account ☐

PRACTICE

3 Read a corrected version of Linda's email. Underline her corrections, and compare your answers with a partner's.

LinSun123@abc.edu
To: David Alcott
Re: Missed classes in History 104

Dear Professor Alcott,

I am in your 10:00 session of History 104. I want to apologize for missing several classes in the last two weeks. I had a problem with my work schedule. I have tried to make up the work that I missed. I did all of the reading, and I borrowed notes from a classmate, but I still have a few questions about the material. Could I come to your office hours tomorrow to discuss them with you?

Sincerely,

Linda Sun

REAL-WORLD APPLICATION

4 Imagine it is the morning of your history test, but you are too sick to take the test. Write an email to your professor. Use Linda's corrected email in Exercise 3 to help you.

5 Work with a partner. Look at your partner's email and make suggestions on how to improve it.

6 Use your partner's feedback to revise your email.

LEARNING OBJECTIVES

Reading skill	Make inferences
Grammar	Phrases and modals to state opinions; transition words and phrases to state purpose
Academic writing skill	Essay structure
Writing Task	Write an opinion essay
On Campus	Avoid procrastination

HEALTH AND FITNESS

ACTIVATE YOUR KNOWLEDGE

Work with a partner. Discuss the questions.

1 Look at the photo. Do you think this is a healthy activity? Why or why not?

2 What are some habits of healthy people?

3 What things do healthy people usually avoid?

4 What kinds of things can people do to get in shape or stay in shape?

PREPARING TO WATCH

ACTIVATING YOUR KNOWLEDGE

1 You are going to watch a video about nutrition. Before you watch, work with a partner and discuss the questions.

1 What do you often eat for a snack?
2 Which snack foods are healthy and which are unhealthy?
3 What information on a nutrition label is important to you?

PREDICTING CONTENT USING VISUALS

2 Work with a partner. Look at the photos from the video and discuss the questions.

1 Which of these foods do you think has the most calories?
2 What do you think the woman with the blond hair is doing in the first photo?
3 What could Michelle Obama be talking about?

GLOSSARY

nutrition label (n) a chart on a package of food that gives information about how the food might affect your health

Food and Drug Administration (n) FDA; the U.S. government agency that makes sure food and medicine is safe for people to use

serving size (n) the amount of a food or drink one person normally eats or drinks at one meal

beverage (n) a drink of any type

consumer (n) someone who buys goods or services for personal use

---

WHILE WATCHING

3 ▶ Watch the video. Match the sentence halves.

1 The FDA wants to
2 The calories on food labels will
3 The serving size will
4 The new labels will
5 Changing food labels could

a be more realistic.
b list any added sugars.
c cost a lot of money.
d change the labels on food.
e be bigger and easier to read.

4 ▶ Watch the video again. Answer the questions.

1 When was the last time food labels were changed?
_____

2 How will serving sizes change?
_____

3 What have some beverage companies already done?
_____

4 How much could it cost to produce new labels?
_____

5 What does Michelle Obama think parents have a right to understand?
_____

5 Work with a partner. Discuss the questions and give reasons for
your answers.

1 Why would a food company not list added sugars?
2 Why would a food company list a serving size that is smaller than
what someone usually eats or drinks?
3 Which of the following would Michelle Obama probably support?
a healthier public school lunches
b smaller labels on snack foods
c higher taxes on beverages

DISCUSSION

6 Work in a small group. Discuss your answers.

1 What is the purpose of nutrition labels on food?
2 What other products have special warning labels? Do warning labels
work? Why or why not?
3 What could you eat more of to become healthier? What could you
eat less of?

READING

PREPARING TO READ

UNDERSTANDING KEY VOCABULARY

1 Read the sentences. Complete the definitions with the words in bold.

1 Type 2 diabetes is an extremely **serious** condition. Many people die each year from the complications of this illness.
2 Participation in sports is an excellent way to raise the **self-esteem** of teenagers. It helps them to feel confident and happy with themselves.
3 My grandmother is 88 years old, but she is still quite **active**. She walks every day and even plays tennis twice a week.
4 To lose weight, you should get more exercise and eat fewer **calories**.
5 To stay healthy you should do a **moderate** amount of exercise each week. Two and a half hours a week is the right amount.
6 Many young people do not **recognize** the importance of getting enough sleep.
7 I have decided to **reduce** the amount of sugar I eat. Now I have dessert only once a week.

a _____ (adj) doing things that involve movement and energy
b _____ (v) to limit; to use less of something
c _____ (adj) bad or dangerous
d _____ (n) a feeling of confidence and pride in yourself
e _____ (n) measurement of the amount of energy found in food
f _____ (v) to understand; to accept that something is true
g _____ (adj) not too much and not too little

PREDICTING CONTENT USING VISUALS

2 Write the names of the types of exercise shown in the photos.

a _____
b _____
c _____
d _____
e _____
f _____
g _____
h _____

1   How much physical activity do you do in a week? Are you getting enough exercise? Regular activity benefits your health in many ways. For example, people who exercise regularly are less likely to suffer from many chronic diseases[1], such as heart disease, type 2 diabetes[2], stroke[3], and some cancers. Experts say adults who exercise for just 150 minutes a week can **reduce** their risk of **serious** illness by 50%. In addition, regular exercise increases life expectancy[4] and reduces the risk of early death by 30%. It also improves your mood, **self-esteem**, and sleep quality.

2   Today, most adults are much less **active** than in the past because our jobs are far less physical than the work our grandparents used to do. In fact, many of us spend seven hours or more just sitting in a chair each day. This lack of regular physical activity means that people burn fewer **calories** than in the past, so we need to make an extra effort to use up all our energy. According to experts, adults need to do two and a half hours of **moderate** exercise per week. This could be fast walking or cycling on a flat road. In addition, it is important to do exercises to strengthen muscles two or three times a week.

3   Exercise can be expensive, but it doesn't have to be. Team sports such as soccer or basketball can be cheap because all the players share the cost of the field or court. Joining a recreational sports league is usually an inexpensive way of getting exercise and can be very social, too. Local recreation centers usually offer racquetball at low rates if you book a court at off-peak times, and you may be able to get a reduced price gym membership, too.

4   If you don't want to spend any money at all, try one of the following activities. Go for a run; the only equipment you need is a pair of running shoes. If you take the bus, try getting off one stop early and walking the extra distance. Go to the park. Try getting a group of friends or family together for a game of soccer, or play the kinds of running games you haven't played since you were a child. This is a great way to involve the whole family and also help you get in shape. Alternatively, if you want to stay at home, gardening or doing housework are great ways to get in shape, and you can enjoy the benefit of a nice garden and a tidy house, too!

5   Although adults should do two and a half hours of exercise a week, you don't have to do it all at one time. Split the time into ten-minute chunks! If you do ten minutes before work, ten minutes during your lunch break and ten minutes after work, five days a week, you've achieved the target! You could also go swimming during your lunch hour two or three times a week and you've done it! In brief, there are many easy ways of getting in shape. If we all **recognize** the value of doing this, we will live longer and be healthier.

[1]**chronic disease** (n) a disease that lasts a long time

[2]**diabetes** (n) a disease in which the body is not able to use sugar efficiently

[3]**stroke** (n) a medical condition in which blood cannot reach the brain and the brain becomes damaged

[4]**life expectancy** (n) the number of years that a person can expect to live

SKIMMING

3 Skim the magazine article and circle the best title.

  a Get Some Exercise and Lose Weight at the Same Time!
  b Walking to Improve Your Health and Mood
  c Stay in Shape—It's Easier than You Think
  d Exercise Every Day to Keep the Doctor Away

READING FOR MAIN IDEAS

4 Read the article. Match the headings to the paragraphs in the article. There is one extra heading that you do not need.

  a But I can't afford gym membership! _____
  b Exercise regularly to stay healthy. _____
  c But I don't have time! _____
  d Swimming is the best form of exercise. _____
  e Get out of your chair! _____
  f Exercise can be free. _____

READING FOR DETAILS

5 Read the article again and answer the questions.

  1 Which four medical problems can be avoided with regular exercise?
  _____ , _____ , _____ , _____

  2 Which other three things does exercise improve?
  _____ , _____ , _____

  3 How much time do some adults spend each day sitting down?
  _____

  4 What do team sport players share the cost of? _____

  5 When should you book a racquetball court for cheap rates?
  _____

  6 What equipment do you need for running? _____

  7 Where should you go to exercise and spend time with your family?
  _____

READING BETWEEN THE LINES

SKILLS

Making inferences

Making inferences means using your knowledge and clues in the text to guess about things that aren't stated in the text but are probably true. For example: *After two miles, Amir could not run another step, but Danya kept going.*

Question: Who is in better shape, Amir or Danya?   **Answer:** Danya

We can tell Danya is in better shape because she "kept going" and Amir "could not run another step."

Readers may make inferences about the characters in a text (their age, attitude, relationship, feelings, etc.). They also make inferences about the writer's purpose, intention, background, or attitude.

6 Read the article again and answer the questions.

1 How do you think exercise improves self-esteem?

_____

2 What do you think is the relationship between regular exercise and life expectancy?

_____

3 Is the article written for adults or for children? How do you know?

_____

DISCUSSION

7 Work with a partner. Discuss the questions.

1 Do you make time to keep fit? What activities do you do?
2 Are sports the best way to keep fit? Why or why not?
3 Is exercise ever a bad thing? Why or why not?

READING 2

PREPARING TO READ

1 Read the definitions. Complete the sentences with the correct form of the words in bold.

> **balanced diet** (n) a daily eating program that has a healthy mixture of different kinds of food
> **campaign** (n) a group of activities designed to motivate people to take action, such as giving money or changing their behavior
> **junk food** (n) food that is unhealthy but quick and easy to eat
> **nutritional** (adj) relating to food and the way it affects your health
> **obesity** (n) the condition of being extremely overweight
> **portion** (n) an amount of food served to one person

1 I try to eat a _____ consisting of a little meat, some dairy products, and a lot of fruit, vegetables, and grains.
2 I love _____ like potato chips and hot dogs, but I'm careful not to eat too much of those foods because I know they aren't good for me.
3 _____ is a serious problem all over the world. In some countries, more than 50% of adults are overweight.
4 One way to lose weight is to eat the same foods but smaller _____ .
5 Right now, my company is sponsoring a _____ to raise money for a new gym in the local school.
6 Snacks like candy and potato chips have little _____ value. Having fruit or raw vegetables is much better for your body.

2 Work with a partner. Answer the questions.

1 What percentage of your diet should be
   a fruit and vegetables? _____
   b carbohydrates? _____
   c dairy products? _____
   d proteins? _____
2 How can governments help people avoid obesity?

   _____

3 Scan the essay on page 111 and check your answers to the questions in Exercise 2.

WHILE READING

4 Read the essay. Match the paragraphs of the essay to the themes.

   a the government's role _____
   b how to have a healthy diet _____
   c nutritional information _____
   d an introduction to the obesity problem _____
   e the role of advertising _____
   f an end to obesity _____

5 Read paragraphs 2–5 of the essay again and make notes on the purpose of each solution to the problem of obesity.

solutions to tackle obesity	purpose
a balanced diet	1 to maintain a healthy weight
packaging labels	2
a food tax	3
a ban on junk food advertising to children	4
education campaigns	5

Tackling obesity

1   **Obesity** is becoming a major problem in many parts of the world. In the United States, the number of obese adults has more than doubled over the past 25 years. Nearly 70% of American adults are overweight or obese. Obesity can cause major health problems like heart disease, diabetes, stroke, and breathing problems. Experts estimate that in the United States alone, 1 in 5 deaths are linked to obesity—that is almost 300,000 deaths per year. Tackling[1] obesity is a big task. In my opinion, it should be the shared responsibility of individuals, governments, and the media.

2   First, individuals need to do their part to make sure they stay healthy. One way for people to fight obesity is to eat smaller **portions** and to eat more healthfully. An average man needs around 2,500 calories per day, while an average woman requires around 2,000. We should eat a **balanced diet** that consists of a variety of foods in order to maintain a healthy weight. A healthy diet should include approximately 50% fruit and vegetables; 30% carbohydrates, such as bread, rice, potatoes, and pasta; 15% proteins, for example, meat, fish, eggs, and beans; and around 5% dairy products, such as milk and cheese. Very little should be sweet foods like candy or cookies.

3   Governments around the world must also do their part to fight obesity in their countries. In many countries, laws require food packaging to show accurate **nutritional** information. In addition, large restaurant chains in the United States must list calorie counts for items on their menus. These restaurants must also provide additional written nutritional information about fat, sodium[2], and cholesterol[3] amounts if a customer asks for it. This information helps people better understand the nutritional value of the food they eat, even when they are not cooking at home or eating packaged food. Some countries tax foods that are high in fat, such as pizza and potato chips, and those high in refined sugar[4], like chocolate and candy. This makes **junk food** too expensive for people to buy in large quantities. In some countries, there is now a tax on products that contain more than a certain percentage of saturated fat[5].

4   Moreover, the role of the media and advertising should not be overlooked. Advertising junk food at times when children are watching TV was banned in Malaysia in 2007. This action was designed to protect children from the influence of advertising while they learn how to choose between treats and foods that are good for them. There have also been several educational **campaigns** on TV to encourage people to eat five portions of fruit and vegetables per day. It has been estimated that if people ate enough fruits and vegetables, up to 2.7 million lives per year could be saved.

5   To summarize, individuals, governments, and the media all need to do their part to reduce obesity in our society. Individuals should take responsibility for their meal choices and choose healthier foods in smaller portions. At the same time, governments should take action and pass laws that encourage healthier lifestyles. The media can also play a role by teaching people about healthier eating habits and not advertising junk food to children. I believe that if individuals, governments, and the media all do their part, then perhaps we can see an end to obesity in the near future.

[1]**tackle** (v) to deal with something
[2]**sodium** (n) the main chemical element found in salt
[3]**cholesterol** (n) a fatty substance found in all animal cells. A high level can block arteries and may cause heart disease.
[4]**refined sugar** (n) white table sugar, which has been processed in a factory, as opposed to the natural sugar found in fruit or honey
[5]**saturated fat** (n) unhealthful fats that contain higher proportions of fatty acid

6 Read the essay again to look for the examples that the author uses to add detail to the argument.

topic	examples
carbohydrates	1 bread
dairy products	2
proteins	3
sweet foods	4
high-fat foods	5
sugary foods	6

READING BETWEEN THE LINES

MAKING INFERENCES

7 Work with a partner. Answer the questions.

1 Why does the author think that obesity is a serious problem?

_____

2 Following the information in the text, give an example of a balanced meal that you ate recently.

_____

3 How does nutritional information on food packaging and in restaurants help people eat more healthfully?

_____

4 Why do you think the government of Malaysia decided to ban junk food advertisements to children? What information did they probably use to support this decision?

_____

DISCUSSION

SYNTHESIZING

8 Work with a partner. Use ideas from Reading 1 and Reading 2 to answer the following questions.

1 Which is more important for good health: a regular exercise program or a balanced diet? Why?

2 Many people work hard and get a lot of exercise in their jobs, but they are still obese. Why do you think that happens?

3 Do you think that advertisements for junk food should be illegal? Why or why not?

4 Do you agree that governments should tax products that are bad for our health? Why or why not?

VERB AND NOUN FORMS

LANGUAGE

It is important to recognize both the verb and the noun form of words when you are reading, and to spell them correctly when you are writing.

Notice: Sometimes the verb and noun forms are the same.

*The biggest thing that stops people going to the gym is the **cost**. (noun)*
*Gym membership should **cost** less so more people can join. (verb)*

1 Look at the verbs in the box and underline their noun forms in the paragraph.

> advertise   ban   encourage   promote
> protect   recognize   reduce

> We need to see a reduction in the rate of obesity among young people. The first step is recognition that fat is a real problem for young people. One solution is for schools to offer children the opportunity to participate in sports. This would require the involvement and encouragement of parents, who are our main weapon against increasing obesity. Parents can also support the promotion of educational campaigns to teach children about healthy eating.
> All of us should be responsible for the protection of our own health, but governments can also help fight the obesity epidemic. For example, they can impose a ban on junk food advertisements that target children.

HEALTH AND FITNESS COLLOCATIONS

Collocations are pairs of words that frequently occur together, for example, noun + noun or adjective + noun. Collocations sound correct to fluent speakers of a language. For example, *heart disease* is a frequent collocation in English. It sounds correct. On the other hand, *heart illness* sounds wrong, even though we can understand the meaning.

PRISM **Online** Workbook

2 Look at the paragraph and underline ten collocations (noun + noun or adjective + noun) related to health and fitness. The first one has been done for you as an example.

> Obesity can reduce <u>life expectancy</u> and lead to serious illness such as heart disease and diabetes. To address this problem, some governments run educational programs and advertising campaigns. These educate people about the dangers of junk food and the importance of a balanced diet. They also show people how to find out about the nutritional value of food. Another important way to tackle obesity is regular exercise, because the more physical activity we have, the better we feel.

3 Now complete the chart by writing the correct collocation next to the definition.

definition	collocation
how long a person can expect to live	1 life expectancy
how good a particular kind of food is for you	2
classes or material to teach people about a particular topic	3
an illness of the heart	4
moving around and doing things	5
media projects to convince people to buy a product or change their behavior	6
a very bad medical problem	7
a mixture of the correct types and amounts of food	8
sports or movement that people do at the same time each day, week, month, etc.	9
food that is unhealthy but is quick and easy to eat	10

WRITING

CRITICAL THINKING

At the end of this unit, you will write an opinion essay. Look at this unit's Writing Task below.

> Should colleges and universities require students to take physical education classes?

SKILLS

Subdividing arguments

When you plan an opinion essay, make a list of arguments. Then, list ideas for or against each argument. This will help you think about your own opinions and how you will support your position.

1 Look back at Reading 2 on page 111. Complete the list of arguments that the author gives and the evidence she uses to support her opinion. Use your own words.

UNDERSTAND ▲

author's opinion: Individuals, governments, and the media should share the responsibility for tackling obesity.	
argument 1:	evidence:
argument 2:	evidence:
argument 3:	evidence:

2 Work with a partner. Look at the writing topic. Make a list of arguments for and against this proposal.

REMEMBER ▲

topic: *Colleges and universities should require students to take physical education classes.*	
arguments in favor	arguments against
Exercise decreases stress.	Students are busy, and physical education classes will take time away from their studies.

APPLY

3 Review your arguments in the chart on page 115. Decide if you will argue for or against the topic. Write your opinion in the chart below.

my opinion:	
argument 1:	evidence:
argument 2:	evidence:
argument 3:	evidence:

4 Look at the arguments and opinions you wrote in Exercise 3. Write evidence that supports each point.

GRAMMAR FOR WRITING

STATING OPINIONS

LANGUAGE

Good writers need to clearly state their opinions when they write an opinion essay. You can state your opinion with opinion phrases or with modals.

opinion phrases	
In my opinion, *In my view,* *I believe (that)* *I think (that)*	**In my opinion,** individuals, governments, and the media should share the responsibility for tackling obesity.
modals	
should / shouldn't *ought to* *need to / don't need to* *must / don't have to*	The media **need to** play a larger role in fighting obesity. Individuals **ought to** make better food choices.

1 Read the questions and answer them with an opinion phrase.

1 Should governments pay for people to enroll in weight reduction programs?

   _____

2 Should junk food advertisements be illegal?

   _____

3 Is running the best exercise for staying in shape?

   _____

4 Do most adults spend too much time sitting?

   _____

5 Is it necessary to sleep eight hours a night in order to stay healthy?

   _____

2 Fill in the blanks with a modal. Use the affirmative or negative form according to your opinion. Use a different expression in each sentence.

1 Children _____ spend more than half an hour each day watching television.
2 School cafeterias _____ sell only healthful food.
3 Cities _____ build parks and playgrounds in every neighborhood.
4 Most people _____ exercise 10 hours a week.
5 In most countries, food packages _____ have labels that provide nutritional information.

STATING A PURPOSE

When you give reasons for your opinions, you can use *to* or *in order to* to indicate purpose. Both are followed by an infinitive.

Governments should promote healthy eating	**to**	increase life expectancy.
	in order to	

You can also use *so* or *so that*. These are usually followed by a clause with *can*.

Governments should build more recreation centers	**so**	people can play more sports.
	so that	

3 Complete the sentences using *to, in order to, so,* or *so that.* In some items, more than one answer is possible.

1 Governments need to increase the tax on junk food _____ make it more expensive.
2 Nutrition labels should be added to food packaging _____ people can see if their food is healthy or not.
3 Governments should provide free sports clubs _____ people living in poorer areas can participate in sports.
4 Governments can promote the idea of eating five portions of fruit and vegetables per day _____ improve people's diets.
5 Some people argue that junk food advertising should be banned _____ children are not influenced by it.

ESSAY STRUCTURE

SKILLS

An essay is a group of paragraphs that discuss one main topic. Essays have three important parts.

- An **introductory paragraph** presents the topic, gives background information, and shows the organization of the essay. The last sentence of the introductory paragraph gives a **thesis statement**, which indicates what the body paragraphs will be about. In an opinion essay, the thesis states the writer's opinion about the topic.

- **Body paragraphs** (usually 2–4) explain or develop the thesis statement. Each body paragraph starts with a topic sentence that links back to the thesis statement. Each body paragraph provides supporting details to its topic sentence.

- A **concluding paragraph** restates the thesis statement and provides the writer's final thoughts on the topic. In an opinion essay, the concluding paragraph restates the writer's opinion and often concludes with a prediction about the future or a recommendation for action.

1 Look back at Reading 2 on page 111. Complete the outline showing the organization of the essay. Write notes; do not copy whole sentences.

PRISM Online Workbook

1	Introductory paragraph
	Topic: *obesity*
	Background: *facts about obesity*
	Thesis statement / author's opinion:
2	Topic sentence:
	Supporting detail: *eat smaller portions*
	Supporting detail:
3	Topic sentence:
	Supporting detail:
	Supporting detail: *restaurants list calorie counts*
	Supporting detail:
4	Topic sentence:
	Supporting detail:
	Supporting detail:
5	Concluding paragraph
	Restatement of thesis:
	Prediction or recommendation:

▶ Should colleges and universities require students to take physical education classes?

PLAN

1 Look at the chart you created in Exercise 3 in Critical Thinking. Use the outline to plan your opinion essay.

introductory paragraph	background information: 1 2 3 thesis statement:
body paragraph 1	argument 1 with supporting details:
body paragraph 2	argument 2 with supporting details:
concluding paragraph	restatement of thesis: prediction or recommendation:

WRITE A FIRST DRAFT

2 Write an essay giving your opinion of the proposal in the Writing Task. Use the plan above to help you. Remember to include an introductory paragraph, two body paragraphs giving your arguments, and a concluding paragraph.

REVISE

3 Use the Task Checklist to review your essay for content and structure.

TASK CHECKLIST	✔
Does your introductory paragraph include background information and a thesis statement?	
Does your thesis statement give your opinion?	
Did you follow the essay plan and include arguments to support your opinion?	
Does your concluding paragraph restate your thesis?	

4 Make any necessary changes to your essay.

EDIT

5 Use the Language Checklist to edit your essay for language errors.

LANGUAGE CHECKLIST	✔
Did you use a range of academic nouns and verbs?	
Did you use health and fitness collocations?	
Did you use opinion phrases or modals for stating your opinion?	
Did you use *to, in order to, so,* and *so that* correctly to state a purpose?	

6 Make any necessary changes to your essay.

ON CAMPUS

AVOIDING PROCRASTINATION

Procrastination, or waiting until the last minute to do something, is a big problem for a lot of students. There are reasons why everyone procrastinates, but there are also strategies to avoid it.

PREPARING TO READ

1 You are going to read a blog about procrastination by an academic counselor. Before you read, work with a partner and discuss the questions.

   1 In what situations do you procrastinate? What do you always do right away?
   2 Why do you think you procrastinate?

WHILE READING

2 Read the blog on the next page. Match the reason for procrastinating with the strategies to avoid procrastination.

   1 A student is easily distracted. _____
   2 A student doesn't understand what to do on an assignment. _____
   3 A student thinks he or she can write the paper very quickly. _____
   4 A project seems very big. _____

   a Start early even if it's a simple task.
   b Ask the professor for help.
   c Write a list of the smaller tasks in the project
   d Study in a place away from friends.

3 Read the blog again. Circle the correct option to complete the sentences.

   1 When students need help with an assignment, they shouldn't feel _____ to ask for it.
      a distracted   b lazy   c embarrassed
   2 After making a list of smaller tasks, a student can also _____ .
      a do the easy ones first   b choose a date to finish each task
      c write a first draft
   3 Sometimes, students are surprised because _____ .
      a the project takes longer than they expected   b they started early
      c their first draft is very easy
   4 Students should not _____ when they are studying.
      a eat snacks   b leave their phone on   c take a break

PROCRASTINATION

Most people procrastinate from time to time. However, some students procrastinate too often. It affects their health and their grades. Let's look at the reasons why people procrastinate and some strategies to change that behavior. Why do people procrastinate?

Reasons	Strategy
1 They don't have the skills or knowledge to do a task or assignment.	Ask for help. Don't be afraid or embarrassed to ask your professor for help. You can also ask TAs, librarians, peer tutors, or even a friend. All of these people want to help you succeed.
2 The project seems too big and they don't know where to start.	Break the big project into small parts. Make a list of all the parts, such as: choose topic, find sources, write introduction, and so on. For each part, make a deadline[1] for yourself.
3 They don't think a task will take very long and they are surprised when it does.	Start early. If the task doesn't take very long, you'll finish early! Just writing a first draft or an outline will make it clear how difficult or easy the task will be.
4 They are constantly distracted[2].	Go to a quiet place to work, turn off your phone, and do not open email or social media. First, find a comfortable place to study but not a place where you will see friends or roommates. Then, turn off your devices and focus on work. You can check those things when you take a break.

If you need help with this or other study problems, come see us in Thompson Hall. But don't wait!
Bert Ryan, Counselor, Student Support Center

[1]**deadline (n)** the day or time something must be finished   [2]**distracted (adj)** unable to pay attention to something

PRACTICE

4 Work with a partner. Discuss the questions.

  1 Which reasons for procrastinating from the reading are true for you?

  2 Which strategies from the reading do you use or will you try to use?

  3 What are some other strategies for avoiding procrastinating?

REAL-WORLD APPLICATION

5 Work with a partner. Survey five students on your campus. Ask these questions.

  1 Do you ever procrastinate?

  2 What do you do when you procrastinate?

  3 How do you avoid procrastinating?

6 Work with another pair. Use the information from the interviews to create a poster with dos and don'ts about procrastination.

7 Share your poster with the class.

Reading skill	Scan to find information
Grammar	Relative clauses; prepositional phrases with advantages and disadvantages
Academic writing skill	Write an introductory paragraph
Writing Task	Write an explanatory essay
On Campus	Annotate texts

DISCOVERY AND
INVENTION

ACTIVATE YOUR KNOWLEDGE

Work with a partner. Discuss the questions.

1 Think of an invention from the last ten years. What does it do?
   What is its purpose? How does it help people? Does it have any
   disadvantages?

2 If you could invent one thing to help the world, what would it be?

3 Look at the photo. What do you think will happen in the world of
   science and technology in the next ten years? Will scenes like this
   become more common?

DISCOVERY AND INVENTION   125

PREPARING TO WATCH

ACTIVATING YOUR KNOWLEDGE

1 You are going to watch a video about a river in China. Before you watch, work with a partner and discuss the questions.

1 What are some inventions to help us control our natural environment?
2 How does water get into your home?
3 How does water become clean enough to drink?

PREDICTING CONTENT USING VISUALS

2 Work with a partner. Look at the photos from the video and discuss the questions.

1 Where do you think the video takes place?
2 What do you think these people are building?
3 What problem could this project solve?

GLOSSARY

canal (n) a man-made river built for boats to travel along or to take water where it is needed

frame (n) the basic structure of a building, vehicle, piece of furniture, etc. that other parts are added onto

concrete (n) a hard substance that is used in building and made by mixing sand, water, small stones, and cement

crane (n) a large, usually tall machine used for lifting and moving heavy things

pump (n) a piece of equipment that pushes liquid or gas somewhere, especially through pipes or tubes

---

WHILE WATCHING

3 ▶ Watch the video. Answer the questions.

1 Where do most of the people in China live? _____

2 What problem does China have? _____

3 How is each section of the canal built? _____

4 Why does the crane operator have to be very careful?

_____

5 When will the project be completed? _____

6 Who will the new canal help? _____

UNDERSTANDING
MAIN IDEAS

4 ▶ Watch the video again. Correct the student notes.

UNDERSTANDING
DETAILS

1	Problem = people in north need food
2	Solution = build a lake
3	Length = 570 miles
4	Weight of each concrete section = 12 tons
5	End of each section = 1 meter higher than other end
6	Finish date = 2020

DISCUSSION

5 Work in a small group. Discuss the questions.

1 List the five most important inventions in the past 100 years.

2 Rank the inventions in your list in order of importance.

3 Complete the chart. Then, compare your answers with another group.

invention	purpose or reason	positive effect	negative effect

READING

PREPARING TO READ

UNDERSTANDING KEY VOCABULARY

1 Read the definitions. Complete the sentences with the correct form of the words in bold.

> **essential** (adj) very important or necessary
> **harmful** (adj) able to hurt or damage
> **helpful** (adj) useful
> **illustrate** (v) to show the meaning or truth of something more clearly, especially by giving examples
> **pattern** (n) a set of lines, colors, or shapes that repeat in a regular way
> **prevent** (v) to stop something from happening or stop someone from doing something
> **unlimited** (adj) without end or restriction

1 Before the invention of sunscreen, people had no way to protect themselves from the _____ rays of the sun.

2 Many cooks say that the food processor was a _____ invention because it saves a lot of preparation time in the kitchen.

3 The discovery of vaccines was extraordinarily important because they make it possible for us to _____ millions of deaths from illnesses like polio and smallpox.

4 The planet Uranus has an interesting _____ of stripes, which is visible by viewing the planet with a telescope.

5 The human brain has an almost _____ memory capacity, far more than that of a computer.

6 If you want to be an engineer or a scientist, it's _____ that you get a strong background in science and math.

7 The engineer used diagrams to _____ his point about the mechanics of suspension bridges like the Golden Gate Bridge.

USING YOUR KNOWLEDGE

2 Work with a partner. Discuss the questions.

1 *Bio-* is a prefix that means "life." What words do you know that start with *bio-*?

2 Read the introduction and the first paragraph of the article on page 129. What do *mimicry* and *biomimicry* mean?

3 Can you think of any inventions that copy their shape or function from something in nature?

THE MAGIC OF MIMICRY

To *mimic* people means "to copy their speech, dress, or behavior." However, in science, *mimic* means "copying ideas from nature or natural processes to solve problems or to create helpful products." This is called *biomimicry*, and its influence can be seen in many everyday products.

1 Perhaps the best-known example of biomimicry is Velcro®. It was invented in 1941 by a Swiss engineer called George de Mestral. One day, Mestral noticed the burdock seeds that stuck to his dog's hair. Under the microscope, he discovered that these seeds had hooks on them, so they stuck to loops on clothing or hair. Mestral copied this idea and created two strips of material, one with tiny hooks and the other with loose loops. When he put both strips together, they stuck like glue. However, unlike with glue, he could peel the strips apart and reattach them. Velcro® was initially unpopular with fashion companies, but after it was used by NASA to stop items from floating in space, it became popular with children's clothing companies. Today it is used to fasten everything from lunch bags to shoes.

2 More recently, swimwear has also been influenced by nature. The Speedo Fastskin®, a controversial swimsuit, was seen at the Beijing Olympics in 2008 and worn by 28 of the 33 gold medal winners. The technology is based on the rough **patterns** on a shark's skin, which allows the shark to swim faster. A shark's skin also **prevents** bacteria from growing on it, so scientists are copying this surface to design cleaner hospitals.

3 For NASA, protecting astronauts' eyes from the sun's rays is very important, but protecting their eyes from other dangerous radiation is also **essential**. Scientists studied how eagles and falcons clearly recognize their prey. Scientists discovered that the birds have yellow oil in their eyes, which filters out **harmful** radiation and allows them to see very clearly. NASA copied this oil, and it is now used by astronauts and pilots in Eagle Eyes® glasses. In addition to protecting eyes from dangerous rays, these sunglasses also improve vision in different weather conditions such as fog, sunlight, or just normal light.

4 To show how biomimicry could be used, Mercedes-Benz developed a concept car that was based on the shape of the tropical boxfish. Opinions were divided about the car's appearance, but the engineers at Mercedes-Benz chose to copy the boxfish skeleton to make their Bionic Car because of its strength and low weight. The boxfish's bony body protects the animal's insides from injury in the same way that a car needs to protect the people inside it. This shape also meant that the car had less air resistance and therefore used less fuel.

5 As these examples **illustrate**, biomimicry appears to have an **unlimited** number of applications. It will be interesting to see which problems nature helps us solve in the future.

READING FOR MAIN IDEAS

3 Read the article. Choose the sentence that best summarizes the main idea of the article.

   a Though sharks can be dangerous, their skin is useful.
   b In the future, nature can help us solve many important problems.
   c Many useful products have been designed using biomimicry.
   d Many useful discoveries have been made by accident.

SKILLS

Scanning to find information

Scanning means reading for specific information. When you scan a text, do not read every word. Look for key words that help you understand what the text is about and specific information. For example, look for names, numbers, pronouns, or groups of words related to a same topic/theme (e.g., words related to spend).

SCANNING TO FIND INFORMATION

PRISM Online Workbook

4 Scan the magazine article on page 129 quickly to answer the questions.

   1 Which products are mentioned in the article?

   _____

   2 Which plants or animals were copied to produce these products?

   _____

ANNOTATING

5 Read the article to find the answers to the questions. Annotate the text as you read. Look at page 85 for what to annotate. Write summary notes in the margin.

   1 Which two features of Velcro® make the strips stick together?
   2 What are some uses of Velcro®?
   3 What product mimics a shark's skin?
   4 What does a shark's skin allow the shark to do?
   5 Whose eyes did NASA want to protect from dangerous radiation?
   6 What special feature of an eagle's eyes was copied to make sunglasses?
   7 Which two features of a boxfish's skeleton make it good for engineers to copy?
   8 What feature does the car copy that allows it to save fuel?

READING BETWEEN THE LINES

MAKING INFERENCES

6 Work with a partner. Answer the questions.

   1 Why do you think Velcro® became popular with children's clothing companies?

   _____

   2 Why do you think the Speedo Fastskin® swimsuit was controversial during the Beijing Olympics?

   _____

   3 Why do people have different opinions about the Bionic Car?

   _____

DISCUSSION

7 Work with a partner. Discuss the questions.

1 Do you think biomimicry will be more common in the future? Why or why not?
2 What are the advantages of copying from nature?

READING 2

PREPARING TO READ

1 You are going to read an article about technology in the future. Before you read the article, read the definitions below. Complete the sentences with the correct form of the words in bold.

UNDERSTANDING
KEY VOCABULARY

PRISM Online Workbook

> **artificial** (adj) not natural; made by people
> **break down** (phr v) to stop working
> **electronic** (adj) sent or accessed by means of a computer or other electronic device
> **movement** (n) a change of position or place
> **object** (n) a thing you can see or touch that isn't alive
> **personal** (adj) belonging or used by just one person
> **power** (n) energy, usually electricity, used to provide heat, light, etc.
> **three-dimensional** (adj) not flat; having depth, length, and width

1 When working on a computer, you should save your work often so that you don't lose your data if the _____ fails.
2 Smartphones allow us to choose what we want to see and use. Each person's phone is very _____ and doesn't look the same as anyone else's.
3 You don't need a paper ticket because I've got an _____ one on my phone.
4 _____ imaging techniques give doctors a new way to view the inside of the human body.
5 The advances in technology for man-made arms and legs allows _____ in all directions so people can continue to live a normal life.
6 Since cell phones were invented, it has been much easier for people to get help if their car _____ on the highway.
7 Microscopes allow us to see _____ that are too small to see with our eyes.
8 _____ legs have become so advanced that people can use them to run in marathons and climb mountains.

2 Work with a partner. Answer the questions.

1 Do you think flying cars will be a reality someday? Why or why not?

_____

_____

2 What is a 3D printer? What is it used for?

_____

_____

3 How can robots help people who are missing arms or legs?

_____

_____

WHILE READING

SCANNING TO FIND
INFORMATION

3 Scan the article on page 133 to answer the questions. Look for the bold phrases in the questions.

1 Which paragraph describes a **robot suit**? _____
2 Which paragraph describes a **flying car**? _____
3 Which paragraph describes a **3D printer**? _____

READING FOR
MAIN IDEAS

4 Read the article and complete the chart with the advantages and disadvantages of each invention.

a The process is slow and expensive.
b We could avoid speeding tickets.
c It could help people walk again.
d Mechanical failure might be a big problem.
e The cost is too high.
f We could make our own plastic products.

invention	advantages	disadvantages
1 flying car		
2 3D printing		
3 a robot suit		

The World of Tomorrow

1   What will the world of the future be like? Will it be easier or more difficult? Many people are confident that technology is going to help solve some of the most challenging problems we have on Earth today. Other people are worried that new technology may solve old problems but create new ones. Here are three predictions about the world of tomorrow.

2   When we dream about the future, many of us like to think that we will be able to exit our garages and take to the skies in our own **personal** flying car. The advantages are obvious. This technology would allow **three-dimensional** freedom of **movement**. We could fly at 480 kilometers per hour, avoiding traffic lights, busy roads, and speeding tickets. However, some people point to the disadvantages of flying cars. They claim that there are certain to be problems with traffic control. If the cars become popular, there is likely to be a problem with air traffic congestion. Another big problem is mechanical failure. What will happen if the cars **break down**? These are problems we must expect if flying cars become a reality.

3   Most of us have printed out an **electronic** document on paper, but think about the possibility of printing out a three-dimensional **object** in plastic. 3D printers build an object using layers of liquid plastic. They build up the layers line by line like a normal printer until the object is complete. Car companies like BMW and Volkswagen already use 3D printers to make life-size models of car parts, and medical technology companies have already used 3D printing to make body parts, such as **artificial** ears. Before long, it might be possible to see a product on a website and then download it to your printer at home. In the future, we could make our own furniture, jewelry, cups, plates, shoes, and toys from designs on our computers. This could be the next big trend in online shopping.

4   Finally, imagine having your own Ironman suit. Several companies are trying to build a practical robot "exoskeleton." This is a suit of robot arms and legs that follows the wearer's movements. It will allow the wearer to lift heavy objects, walk long distances and even punch through walls! There are obvious military advantages for this technology, but there are also benefits for people with disabilities. The suit might help people walk again after disease or injury. However, the obvious disadvantage at the moment is cost. Even a simple exoskeleton can cost hundreds of thousands of dollars. Another problem is battery life. A suit like this needs a lot of **power**; at the moment, the batteries last only about 15 minutes. One other problem is that a badly programed robot suit could injure the wearer. You wouldn't want your robot leg or arm bending the wrong way, for instance.

5   In the future, although we might be able to fly to work, print out a new pair of shoes, or lift a car above our heads, there are plenty of problems to solve before all of this will be possible. In the meantime, we can dream!

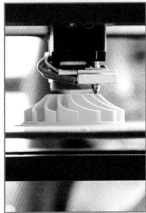

5 Read the article again and write *T* (true), *F* (false), or *DNS* (does not say) next to the statements. Then, correct the false statements.

_____ 1 Flying cars will allow us to avoid traffic congestion on the roads.

_____

_____ 2 Mechanical failure will not be a problem for flying cars.

_____

_____ 3 We might be able to print things like necklaces or chairs in the future.

_____

_____ 4 3D printing was invented in 1984.

_____

_____ 5 BMW and Volkswagen are going to use 3D printing soon.

_____

_____ 6 Robot suits are heavy objects.

_____

_____ 7 The battery life of a robot suit is short at the moment.

_____

READING BETWEEN THE LINES

6 Work with a partner. Answer the questions.

1 Why is mechanical failure a possible problem in a flying car?

_____

2 Why will flying cars cause traffic congestion instead of reducing it?

_____

3 What do you think could be the benefits of robot suits?

_____

4 Why wouldn't you want a robot suit arm to bend the wrong way?

_____

DISCUSSION

7 Work with a partner. Use ideas from Reading 1 and Reading 2 to answer the following questions.

1 Consider all the inventions in Reading 1 and Reading 2. Imagine the year is 2025.
   • Which inventions do you think you will use regularly? Why?
   • Which inventions are no longer used because something better has replaced them?
   • Which inventions failed because they had too many problems?
2 Choose one of the inventions. How would your life be different if you owned it?

MAKING PREDICTIONS WITH MODALS AND ADVERBS OF CERTAINTY

Use *will*, *could*, and *won't* with an adverb of certainty before the main verb to talk about future predictions. For example:

100% = *will definitely*
Cars **will definitely** become more efficient in the future.

90% = *will probably*
The next generation **will probably** use more digital devices.

50% = *could possibly*
We **could possibly** see humans walking on Mars soon.

20% = *probably won't*
We **probably won't** have flying cars.

0% = *definitely won't*
We **definitely won't** be traveling to other stars.

PRISM **Online** Workbook

1 Complete the sentences about the future using modal and adverb phrases with the meaning in parentheses.

   1 In years to come, biofuels _____ become more important. (100%)
   2 Genetic modification _____ be very controversial before the end of the decade. (30%)
   3 In the near future, electronic human implants _____ become very common. (90%)
   4 Biomimicry _____ be a growing industry before too long. (90%)
   5 Robotic cars _____ be everyday products within the next ten years. (100%)
   6 Everyone _____ own a personal Ironman suit within two years. (0%)
   7 By 2020, many people _____ have a 3D printer in their homes. (50%)

2 Look again at Exercise 1 and underline the phrases that refer to future time.

PREFIXES

Prefixes are added to the beginning of a word to make a new word with a different meaning. Understanding the meaning of prefixes can help you guess the general meaning of difficult academic or technical words.

PRISM Online Workbook

3 Look at these prefixes, their meanings, and the examples. Add your own examples to the chart.

prefix	meaning	example
de-	reverse or go down	decrease, _____ , _____
dis-	reverse or opposite	disagree, _____ , _____
en-	cause	enable, _____ , _____
pre-	before	prevent, _____ , _____
re-	again	rebuild, _____ , _____
trans-	across, through	transportation, _____ , _____
un-	remove, reverse, not	unlikely, _____ , _____

4 Compare the pairs of sentences. Use the chart above and write whether the sentences have the same or opposite meanings.

1 Flying cars are **unsafe**.
   Flying cars are dangerous. _____
2 We have to **rethink** the way we use technology.
   We have to think again about how we use technology. _____
3 Genetic engineering **dehumanizes** us.
   Genetic engineering makes us more human. _____
4 Can this software **translate** a document from French to English?
   Can this software change the language of a document from French to English? _____
5 Seat belts in cars **prevent** many injuries and deaths.
   Seat belts cause many injuries and deaths. _____
6 This laboratory is very **disorganized**.
   This laboratory is neat. _____
7 The font on your presentation is too small. Can you **enlarge** it?
   Can you make it bigger? _____

5 Work with a partner. Choose words from the chart above and make five predictions about new technology.

WRITING

CRITICAL THINKING

At the end of this unit, you will write an explanatory essay. Look at the unit's Writing Task below.

> Choose a new area of technology or invention and discuss its advantages and disadvantages.

T-charts

A T-chart is a kind of graphic organizer. It is useful for examining two sides or aspects of a topic, such as advantages/disadvantages or pros/cons. Look at the example.

Invention: tablet computers	
advantages	disadvantages
lightweight portable fast start-up	no physical keyboard too small for working on multiple documents uncomfortable to use for long periods of time

1 Look back at Reading 2 on page 133. Choose one invention from the reading. Complete the T-chart with its advantages and disadvantages.

UNDERSTAND ▲

invention: _____	
advantages	disadvantages

2 Work with a partner. Brainstorm recent inventions in each area of technology below.

areas of technology	inventions
medicine	CT scanner, insulin pump
home	
space	
transportation	
entertainment	
computers	
agriculture	

APPLY

3 Choose one of the inventions from your chart in Exercise 2. Fill in the T-chart with advantages and disadvantages of this invention.

invention: _____

advantages	disadvantages

GRAMMAR FOR WRITING

RELATIVE CLAUSES

Use relative clauses to give more information about a noun without starting a new sentence. There are two kinds of relative clauses: identifying and nonidentifying. Identifying clauses give essential information about the identity of the noun they modify. They are not separated from the rest of the sentence with commas. In contrast, nonidentifying relative clauses have commas before and sometimes after them. They give extra, nonessential information about the noun. These clauses can be removed from the sentence, but the identity of the noun will still be clear.

identifying clauses	
start with *who* for people or *that* for people or things	Velcro® has a unique **structure**. It allows two strips to stick together. → Velcro® has a unique structure **that** <u>allows two strips to stick together</u>.
nonidentifying clauses	
start with *who* for people and *which* for things	Velcro® was invented in 1941 by George de Mestral. **George de Mestral** saw the seeds on his dog's hair. → Velcro® was invented in 1941 by George de Mestral, **who** <u>saw the seeds on his dog's hair</u>.

1 Join each pair of sentences to make one sentence with a relative clause. Add commas if necessary.

1 Scientists have already developed new robots. New robots are able to do dangerous work.

_____

2 There is a great deal of technology to help elderly people. Elderly people may have trouble doing some tasks by themselves.

_____

3 There is a huge amount of new investment in biofuels. Biofuels are cleaner and more sustainable than fossil fuels.

_____

4 The Bionic Car has a special design. A special design makes it more fuel efficient.

_____

5 Important research is being done by scientists at the University of Cambridge. Scientists at the University of Cambridge hope to publish its results next year.

_____

PREPOSITIONAL PHRASES WITH ADVANTAGES AND DISADVANTAGES

Writers often use prepositional phrases at the start of a new sentence to introduce the advantages and disadvantages of a subject.

PRISM Online Workbook

2 Complete the chart with the phrases in bold.

1 The main **advantage of** ... is ...
2 The main **disadvantage of** ... is ...
3 The main **worry about** ... is ...
4 One **point against** ... is ...
5 One **good thing about** ... is ...
6 One **bad thing about** ... is ...
7 Perhaps the biggest **concern with** ... is
8 A real **benefit of** ... is ...
9 The main argument **in favor of** ... is ...
10 The main argument **against** ... is ...
11 The **problem with** ... is ...

positive arguments	negative arguments

3 Choose a negative or positive phrase from Exercise 3 to complete each sentence. More than one answer is possible.

1 _____ robots is that they can do dangerous or boring jobs instead of humans.

2 _____ genetic engineering is that the new plant species may change human DNA.

3 _____ medical imaging is that you can see clearly inside patients' bodies.

4 _____ robots is that they take jobs away from people.

5 _____ flying cars is that they could crash, causing terrible accidents.

ACADEMIC WRITING SKILLS

WRITING AN INTRODUCTORY PARAGRAPH

SKILLS

The first, or introductory, paragraph of an essay usually has three parts:

- a hook
- background information
- a thesis statement

The **hook** is a statement or question at the beginning of the paragraph. Its purpose is to get the reader interested in the topic so he or she will want to keep reading. A good hook can be a thought-provoking question, a surprising fact or statistic, a request to the reader to imagine a situation, an observation, or a quotation. For example:

In 2014, Americans spent 6.9 billion hours sitting in rush-hour traffic. Now imagine what we could do with all that time if we did not need to commute.

Many nations are in danger of running out of water. However, an Israeli company has invented a device that turns water vapor from the air into water you can drink.

Background information provides context to help readers understand the essay. Background information can include a definition of terms, historical information, data and statistics, or a general explanation of the topic.

The **thesis statement** is usually the last sentence of the introduction. It tells the reader how the essay will be developed. Often a thesis statement has two parts: a topic and a point of view. For example:

    topic   point of view

Flying cars may reduce congestion on the ground, but they may create additional problems, such as congestion in the air and pollution.

This thesis statement informs the reader that the topic, flying cars, will be followed by both advantages and disadvantages of flying cars.

1 Read the introduction and the first paragraph of "The Magic of Mimicry" on page 129 again. Answer the questions.

PRISM Online Workbook

  1 What is the hook? Does it get your attention?

       _____

  2 What kind of background information does the paragraph include?

       _____

  3 According to the thesis statement, what is the topic of the essay? What is the point of view? How many paragraphs will the body of the essay probably have? What will each paragraph probably discuss?

       _____

       _____

2 Now re-read the introductory paragraph in "The World of Tomorrow" on page 133. Answer the questions.

1 What is the hook? Does it get your attention?

_____

2 What kind of background information does the paragraph include?

_____

3 According to the thesis statement, what is the topic of the essay? What is the point of view? How many paragraphs will the body of the essay probably have? What will each paragraph probably discuss?

_____

_____

4 Which introduction is better, in your opinion? Why?

_____

WRITING TASK

PRISM ^{Online} Workbook

Choose a new area of technology or invention and discuss its advantages and disadvantages.

_____

PLAN

1 Look at the chart you created in Exercise 3 in Critical Thinking.

2 Plan your essay's introductory paragraph. Write notes on the following parts of the introduction.

Hook:

_____

Background information:

_____

Thesis statement:

_____

3 Outline the body of your essay. How many paragraphs will it have? Make sure the number of paragraphs matches the point of view in your thesis statement. Be sure to include advantages and disadvantages.

_____

_____

_____

_____

_____

_____

_____

_____

4 Plan your concluding paragraph. It should repeat your thesis statement and make a prediction about the future.

_____

_____

5 Use the Task Checklist below as you prepare your essay.

WRITE A FIRST DRAFT
6 Write the first draft of your essay using your essay plan.

REVISE
7 Use the Task Checklist to review your essay for content and structure.

TASK CHECKLIST	✔
Did you write about advantages and disadvantages?	
Did you include an introductory paragraph that has a hook, background information, and a thesis statement?	
Does the number of paragraphs in the body match the point of view in the thesis statement?	
Do the main body paragraphs have a topic sentence, supporting sentences, and a concluding sentence?	
Does the concluding paragraph repeat the thesis statement and make a prediction about the future?	

8 Make any necessary changes to your essay.

EDIT
9 Use the Language Checklist to edit your essay for language errors.

LANGUAGE CHECKLIST	✔
Did you use modals and adverbs of certainty to make predictions about the future?	
Did you use _who, that,_ and _which_ correctly in sentences with relative clauses? Did you use commas correctly?	
Did you introduce advantages and disadvantages with prepositional phrases?	

10 Make any necessary changes to your essay.

ANNOTATING TEXTS

PREPARING TO READ

1 You are going to read a blog from the Peer Tutoring Center. Before you read, work with a partner and discuss the question.

    1 As you read a textbook, what do you do when you ...

      a see new vocabulary?   **c** have questions about the text?

      b have ideas or opinions about   **d** identify important information? the text?

 West Bridge College Peer Tutoring Center

ANNOTATING

Annotating is writing in a text to organize or explain that text. It can include underlining and circling words, or making notes in the margins, like personal comments, questions, or symbols.

Why should I annotate my text?

Learning to annotate your textbooks will help you anytime you need to review for a test, class discussion, or even a project in class. Imagine you have a test that covers three chapters. You've already read the chapters but you don't have time to read them again. If the text is annotated, you can quickly review the most important points.

How do I annotate my text?

1 Use a pencil in case you want to make changes.

- Main ideas: Underline the main ideas. Put a star in the margin.
- Key words: Circle key words. Use these for an Internet search later.
- New words: Put a box around new words.
- Definitions: Write *def.* in the margin if there is a definition of a new word in the text.
- Lists and processes: Add numbers for items in a list or steps in a process.

2 Use a system that you like. Below are some suggestions:

- Details: Write symbols, abbreviations, or words to explain why details are important. Examples: + and − for advantage and disadvantage; *ex.* for example.
- Questions: Write your questions in the margin. Ask your professor or TA about them.
- Comments: Write your own ideas or opinions in the margin.
- Summary: Write a short summary at the end of a section or chapter.

WHILE READING

2 Read the blog. Write *T* (true) or *F* (false) next to the statements. Underline where you found the information in the text.

_____ **1** Annotated texts are helpful for reviewing quickly for a test.

_____ **2** It's a good idea to write your comments with a pen.

_____ **3** All students should learn to annotate in the same way.

_____ **4** Your own ideas or opinions are also part of an annotation.

_____ **5** It's a good idea to write a summary at the bottom of each page.

PRACTICE

3 Look at the annotated text. Complete each sentence below with the correct word or phrase from the box.

| causes | definition | effect | example | key word | question |

> Cause ①
>
> The main causes of (deforestation) are commercial
>
> Cause ②
> farming by big business and farming by local people.
>
> Huge commercial farms have taken over large areas
>
> ex.
> of forest in many countries. In Brazil, for example,
>
> large areas of the Amazon rainforest are cleared to
>
> grow soya and vegetable oil. However, after two or
>
> three years, the land can no longer be used, so the
>
> *How can*
> *they afford* →farmer moves to another piece of land. Normally it
> *to do this?*
> *Do they own* takes around ten years for cleared land to recover,
> *the land?*
> effect ①
> but in populated areas, the land is never allowed to
>
> recover. This constant reuse of land leads to heavy
>
> effect ②
> *def.* erosion—the loss of the top layer of soil that protects
>
> effect
> the ground. Erosion, in turn, can cause flooding in ③
>
> heavy rain.

1 Indonesia is one _____ of commercial agriculture.
2 The reader marks the word "erosion" because the text includes
   a _____ .
3 "Deforestation" is an example of a _____ .
4 The reader indicates that flooding is one _____ of deforestation.
5 The reader includes a _____ about the movement of farmers.
6 In the first sentence, the reader underlines two _____ .

REAL-WORLD APPLICATION

4 Work with a partner. Look at the article "The World of Tomorrow" on page 133 and annotate the following:

- the predictions that the author makes
- the important details in **paragraph 2**
- an example in **paragraph 3**
- a definition in **paragraph 4**

LEARNING OBJECTIVES

Reading skill	Distinguish fact from opinion
Grammar	Multiword prepositions
Academic writing skill	Body paragraphs in argumentative essays; cohesion
Writing Task	Write an argumentative essay
On Campus	Use Internet sources

ACTIVATE YOUR KNOWLEDGE

Work with a partner. Discuss the questions.

1 Which clothing companies are popular in your country? Why are they popular?

2 Why do people buy designer clothing?

3 Do you prefer designer clothing or clothes that are not designer? Why or why not?

4 Are stores that sell cheap clothes popular in your country?

PREPARING TO WATCH

ACTIVATING YOUR KNOWLEDGE

1 Work with a partner. Discuss the questions.

1 Look at the clothes you have on now. Where were they made? Who do you think made them?
2 Describe formal clothes for men and women in your country.
3 If you could have one item of clothing specially made just for you, what would that be?

PREDICTING CONTENT USING VISUALS

2 Work with a partner. Look at the photos from the video and discuss the questions.

1 What industry do you think the men work in?
2 Do you think these clothes are made by machine or by hand?
3 Where would people wear clothes like these?

GLOSSARY

dressed to the nines (idm) wearing fashionable or formal clothes for a special occasion

mow the lawn (v phr) to cut an area of grass, especially near a house or in a park, to keep it short

fabric (n) cloth; material made from cotton, wool, etc., and used to make clothes, curtains, etc.

bespoke tailor (n) a person who makes or sells clothing that is specially made for the customer

client (n) a customer; someone who pays someone else for services

elegantly (adv) in a stylish and beautiful way

WHILE WATCHING

3 ▶ Watch the video. Number the notes in order (1–6).

a	father and son talk _____
b	man signs his name on drawing of a suit _____
c	2 men look at the inside of a jacket _____
d	man cuts material with scissors _____
e	man puts on black jacket _____
f	man looks closely at the material of a jacket _____

4 ▶ Watch the video again. Check the clothes you see.

1 ☐ hat   5 ☐ shoes
2 ☐ jacket   6 ☐ sweater
3 ☐ pants   7 ☐ tie
4 ☐ shirt   8 ☐ winter coat

5 Work with a partner. Discuss the questions and give reasons for your answers.

1 Does the designer prefer formal or informal clothes?
2 Do you think his company makes a large number of jackets each year?
3 How do you think the speaker feels about the way many young people dress today?
4 What does the speaker mean when he says that he wants his clients to step out of their comfort zone?

DISCUSSION

6 Work in a small group. Discuss your answers.

1 When do you wear formal clothes? Do you feel or act differently when you are wearing formal clothes?
2 Do you own any handmade clothes? If so, do you feel differently about them than about items that are made by machines?
3 Besides clothes, what other items do you own that are made by hand? Are they better than items made by machines? Why or why not?

READING

PREPARING TO READ

UNDERSTANDING KEY VOCABULARY

1 You are going to read an article about fashion. Read the sentences. Complete the definitions with the correct form of the words in bold.

1 When you shop for clothes, do you search for specific **brands**, or do you just buy what you like?
2 When a clothing company raises its prices, it is not unusual for the company's sales **volume** to fall.
3 Everyone was talking about the new designer **collections** at the spring fashion show in Milan.
4 My favorite store just launched their new coats for the fall **season**.
5 **Cotton** clothes are cool and soft, but they wrinkle easily.
6 These days, many clothing companies **manufacture** their clothes in Vietnam, Cambodia, or other countries in Southeast Asia.
7 New companies have to **invest** millions of dollars in building factories and training employees.

a _____ (n) a time of year when particular things happen
b _____ (v) to make goods in a large quantity in a factory
c _____ (n) amount of something, especially when it is large
d _____ (n) a group of new clothes produced by a fashion house
e _____ (n) a plant with white fibers used for making cloth
f _____ (v) to use money for the purpose of making a profit, for example, by building a factory
g _____ (n) the name of a product or group of products made by a company

USING YOUR KNOWLEDGE

2 Work with a partner. Answer the questions.

1 What does the term *fast fashion* mean to you?

_____

2 How often do fashions usually change?

_____

3 If fashion designers changed fashions every month, what effect would this have on shoppers? On the clothing industry?

_____

3 Read the article on page 151 and check your answers.

Is *fast fashion* taking over?

1   The fashion industry has changed significantly in recent years. Traditionally, fashion retailers[1] created two clothing **collections** per year, called **seasons**. Each season was a collection of clothes for spring/summer and fall/winter. Nowadays, in contrast, they can design and **manufacture** clothes in as little as four weeks. *Fast fashion* means that the latest designs shown at the fashion shows in Paris, London, New York, and Milan can be copied and sold in shopping malls within a month. A typical fast-fashion retailer can stock 10,000 designs annually, compared with 2,000 for its high-fashion competitors. The largest fast-fashion retailers have annual sales in the billions of dollars.

2   The advantages of rapidly changing fashions are clear. Shortening the life cycle of a product means that if a design doesn't sell well within a week, it is taken out of the stores and replaced with a new one. This is good for manufacturers as it means a greater **volume** of sales. It is also good for customers, who can keep up with fast-moving trends cheaply and who can enjoy finding something new every time they visit the store.

3   However, there are also a number of disadvantages to the fast-fashion approach. Perhaps the biggest concern is the impact of wasted clothes on the environment. The low cost of most fast fashion enables shoppers to buy several new sets of clothes each season instead of wearing the same outfits year after year. This means that huge amounts of clothing are thrown away. Furthermore, with fashions changing so quickly, **cotton** growers need to produce more cotton more cheaply, and that means using more pesticides and chemicals. A third problem is the theft of ideas. Fashion houses **invest** a lot of time and money in new designs, only to see these ideas stolen and copied by fast-fashion companies.

4   Fast fashion rests at one end of the fashion scale. At the other end is high-end designer clothing, where major changes are also happening. At the same time as fast fashion is becoming more and more popular, wealthy consumers worldwide are buying more and more expensive, luxury **brands**. Many well-off customers buy designer clothes just to show that they can afford them, but others choose luxury brands for their quality, saying that they will last longer. They have a point. Due to their longer lifespan, expensive designer clothes are more environmentally friendly.

5   In short, these days it seems that the fashion industry is changing almost as fast as the fashion it produces—but what do you think? We would like to hear your comments about the fashion industry today.

Comments
6 comments

Carmen   Reply

I'd love to have the money to buy designer clothes, but I have to buy cheaper products because I don't have much money. I'm sure the quality is not as good as clothes with designer labels.

👍 Like 14

Ahmet   Reply

Designer fashion is a waste of money. Wearing brand names is just free advertising for that company, and I don't think the quality is any different.

👍 Like 13

[1]**retailer** (n) someone who sells products to people

Jasmine   Reply

Great article!
I love fast fashion! I enjoy looking good and having lots of clothes.
Fast fashion allows me to buy lots of clothes really cheaply. Why
should I feel bad about throwing away cheap clothes when they go
out of fashion? I can just go out and get more.

👍 Like 0

Ben   Reply
Response to Jasmine
People like you make me really angry. That is such a selfish attitude. Think
about the environment. Don't you care about wasting all those clothes? At least
donate the clothes to charity if you don't want them anymore.

👍 Like 7

Sara   Reply

Style is important to me. I study fashion at college and I would
never buy fast fashion. I don't want to look like everyone else. I
prefer to buy secondhand clothes because older clothes were
designed to last. I have my own style. I don't need to copy
Paris or Milan.

👍 Like 11

Fatima   Reply

I can understand why people like fast fashion, but I prefer to pay
for quality, and if the store has ethically produced clothes then
that is perfect. I agree with Ben: we need to take care of the planet;
otherwise, our children won't have a planet to live on. I would rather
pay more and know I'm helping to protect the Earth.

👍 Like 31

WHILE READING

**READING FOR
MAIN IDEAS**

4 Read the article again and number the main ideas in the order that they
are mentioned. Not all the ideas are mentioned. Remember that you can
annotate the article as you read.

a designer clothing _____
b advantages of fast fashion _____
c fast fashion shows _____
d the definition of *fast fashion* __1__
e disadvantages of fast fashion _____

5 Look at the article again and correct the factual mistakes in the sentences. The first one has been done for you as an example.

   1 Traditional fashion retailers annually produce 10,000 designs.
     Traditional fashion retailers annually produce 2,000 designs.

   2 High-end fashion designs that are unpopular are withdrawn in less than a month.

    _____

   3 Traditional fashion is good for the manufacturer because of the greater volume of sales.

    _____

   4 The biggest problem with fast fashion is the theft of ideas.

    _____

   5 Cotton growers need to produce more, so they have to use less fertilizer.

    _____

   6 Designer clothing is popular with middle-class shoppers.

    _____

READING BETWEEN THE LINES

6 Look at the comments about the article and answer the questions.

   1 Who is against designer fashion? _____
   2 Who would like to buy more expensive clothes? _____
   3 Who doesn't like to follow fashion trends? _____
   4 Who has the most likes? Why?

    _____

   5 Who has the fewest likes? Why?

    _____

DISCUSSION

7 Work with a partner. Discuss the questions.

   1 Do you have any fast-fashion clothing stores in your country? If so, which ones?
   2 Do you shop at fast-fashion stores? How often? What do you buy?
   3 Which comment from the reading do you agree with the most? Why?
   4 Is fashion more important to younger or older people? Why?

UNDERSTANDING
KEY VOCABULARY

PRISM Online Workbook

PREPARING TO READ

1 Read the definitions. Complete the sentences with the correct form of the words in bold.

conditions (n) the physical environment where people live or work
import (v) to buy a product from another country and bring it into your country
multinational (adj) referring to a business or company that has offices, stores, or factories in several countries
offshore (adj) located in another country
outsource (v) to have work done by another company, often in another country, rather than in your own company
textile (n) cloth or fabric that is made by crossing threads under and over each other
wage (n) money that people earn for working

1 Some _____ companies are so big that they have branches in more than a hundred countries.
2 Designers at famous fashion houses can earn high _____ .
3 The workers at that factory are well-paid, and their working _____ are safe and comfortable.
4 Scotland is famous for producing beautiful wool _____ , which are often used to make a skirt for men called a kilt.
5 At one time, the company made all its products in the United States. In recent years, however, it decided to _____ its production to Singapore.
6 Many manufacturers do large parts of their production in _____ factories because materials and labor are cheaper in other countries.
7 We _____ fabric from China, then we sew and finish the shirts here.

USING YOUR
KNOWLEDGE

2 Work with a partner. Discuss the questions.

1 Why do some companies outsource their production to other countries?
2 What are the benefits for a country when a multinational company moves its production there?
3 Are there any disadvantages for workers when multinational companies base their factories in their countries?

OFFSHORE PRODUCTION

1   The world's consumption of fashion is huge. To give just one example, the United States alone **imported** almost 122 billion dollars' worth of **textiles** in 2014. As consumption has risen, prices have fallen. Today, a hand-finished shirt may cost as little as five dollars. To make clothes at these low prices, companies have to keep costs down. They use **offshore** production to do this. Large **multinational** companies **outsource** their production to developing countries like Egypt or Cambodia, where workers are paid much less than in developed countries. Supporters of outsourcing claim that it helps local economies, but I believe it is harmful for two main reasons.

2   First, overseas workers usually receive very low **wages**. These workers, many of them women and children, often work 14 hours a day and earn less than a hundred dollars a month. One study of 15 countries found that textile workers earned less than 40% of the money they needed to live on each month. In some countries this figure is even lower. Also, most workers are paid by the piece. This means they might earn only a few cents for making a dress that sells for hundreds of dollars in the United States or Europe. Such low wages are wrong and unfair. As Priya Kapoor, a human rights researcher in Delhi, says, "Garment workers in countries like India and Bangladesh can't afford to pay their basic needs like food and healthcare. We need to establish a fair wage for the work they do."

3   The second problem with outsourcing is that working **conditions** in many offshore factories are uncomfortable and unsafe. It is a fact that worker-protection laws like those in developed nations either don't exist or often are not followed. As a result, workers are exposed to chemicals, dust, and unsafe levels of noise from sewing machines. I saw this myself when I visited a clothing factory in Bangladesh in 2015. The noise was so loud that I had to cover my ears. Moreover, factory buildings are often unsafe, and horrible accidents happen. For example, the whole world was shocked in 2012 when a fire broke out at a garment factory in Dhaka, Bangladesh, that killed 117 people and injured 200.

4   I realize some experts, like the economist David Schneider, say that outsourcing benefits local economies by providing jobs at higher wages than local workers can make by working in agriculture. Supporters of outsourcing point out that people in developing countries often line up to take jobs in multinational factories. These arguments may be correct, but in my opinion they do not justify the low wages and dangerous conditions found in many overseas factories today. If multinationals are going to continue to benefit from low production costs by using overseas suppliers, I believe they should contribute a much larger share of their massive profits to correcting these problems and improving social conditions in the countries where they are located—starting today.

WHILE READING

3 Skim the title and the first paragraph of the essay.

SKIMMING

1 What is the essay about?

_____

2 What is the writer's point of view about this? How do you know?

_____

4 Read the article and match the ideas in the box to the paragraphs. The first one has been done for you as an example. Some paragraphs have more than one answer. Remember that you can annotate the article as you read.

> benefits of outsourcing to local economies
> definition of *outsourcing*   improving social conditions
> overseas wages   ~~volume of textile imports~~
> working conditions in overseas factories

1	volume of textile imports
2	
3	
4	

SCANNING TO FIND
INFORMATION

5 Complete the sentences with words from the article.

1 In 2014, the United States imported almost _____ dollars' worth of textiles.

2 _____ companies outsource their factories to countries where workers are paid less than they are in developed countries.

3 One study found that workers in offshore factories earned only _____ percent of the money they needed each month, even though they worked 14 hours a day.

4 In developing countries, worker-protection laws often _____ .

5 _____ people died in the Dhaka fire in 2012.

6 David Schneider is an _____ .

READING BETWEEN THE LINES

Distinguishing fact from opinion

When you read a text, you need to be able to decide which points are facts and which points are opinions. A *fact* is a true statement that can be proven. An *opinion* usually expresses a person's idea, judgment, or position. In fact, speakers and writers often use facts and reasons to support their opinions and make them sound convincing.

6 Look at the sentences from Reading 2. Check whether they are facts or the writer's opinion.

PRISM Online Workbook

	fact	writer's opinion
1 ... the United States alone imported almost 122 billion dollars' worth of textiles in 2014.		
2 Supporters of outsourcing claim that it helps local economies, but I believe it is harmful for two main reasons.		
3 ... most workers are paid by the piece. This means they might earn only a few cents for making a dress that sells for hundreds of dollars in the United States or Europe.		
4 ... worker-protection laws like those in developed nations either don't exist or often are not followed.		
5 ... working conditions in many offshore factories are uncomfortable and unsafe.		
6 These arguments may be correct, but in my opinion they do not justify the low wages and dangerous conditions found in many overseas factories today.		

DISCUSSION

7 Work with a partner. Use ideas from Reading 1 and Reading 2 to answer the following questions.

1 These days the production of both designer fashion and fast fashion is outsourced to factories in developing countries. Do you think workers make more money if they are producing designer fashions? Do you think there is any difference in working conditions, depending on the type of fashion local workers are making?

2 Read the opinions in Exercise 6. Do you agree or disagree with them? Explain your opinion.

3 After reading the arguments in Reading 2, do you support or oppose overseas production of clothing? Which arguments support your position?

4 Do you think that multinationals that outsource their factories to developing countries should do more for the local community? What should they do?

VOCABULARY FOR THE FASHION BUSINESS

1 Read the sentences. Complete the definitions with the correct form of the words in bold.

1 One of the biggest costs for retailers is **advertising**, but without it, customers have no way of getting information about stores and products.

2 Smart **consumers** shop for clothes during the off-season. For example, they buy winter coats in the spring.

3 Some shoppers only buy clothes made by **designer labels**. If it's not Gucci® or Prada®, they are not interested.

4 In the United States, Forever 21® and H&M® are **competitors**. They have similar prices and they try to attract similar customers.

5 In the clothing business, very little **manufacturing** is done in the United States. Most companies have their factories in other countries.

6 China and India are the two biggest **suppliers** of cotton in the world. Every big clothing company buys from them.

7 In some countries, workers are paid only 14 cents an hour for their **labor**.

8 As well as clothing companies, computer companies also find it cheaper to make their products **overseas**, mainly in Asia.

a _____ (n) a person or company that sells a product or service

b _____ (n) a company that makes or designs expensive clothes

c _____ (adv) in, from or to a country located across the ocean

d _____ (n) a person who buys things to use

e _____ (n) the business of creating or sending out announcements in magazines, on television, etc. to attract shoppers

f _____ (n) businesses that try to win or do better than other businesses selling almost the same products

g _____ (n) work

h _____ (n) the process of making things, especially in a factory

WRITING

CRITICAL THINKING

At the end of this unit, you will write an argumentative essay. Look at this unit's Writing Task in the box below.

> The fashion industry is harmful to society and the environment.
> Do you agree or disagree?

Identifying strong arguments

An *argument* is an opinion that is given with reasons and evidence to prove that the opinion is valid. Successful arguments make the reader understand and recognize that the writer's opinion has some value. A good argument may also convince the reader to agree.

Writers use many types of evidence to support arguments. The most common ones are facts, statistics, quotations, examples, and personal experience.

1 Look at Reading 2 on page 155 and complete the chart with the arguments that the writer uses. You do not need to write complete sentences.

UNDERSTAND

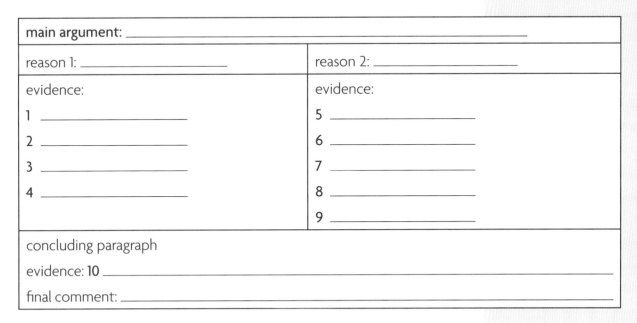

main argument: _____	
reason 1: _____	reason 2: _____
evidence: 1 _____ 2 _____ 3 _____ 4 _____	evidence: 5 _____ 6 _____ 7 _____ 8 _____ 9 _____
concluding paragraph evidence: 10 _____ final comment: _____	

2 Work with a partner. Review the arguments, reasons, and evidence for each point. Based on the reasons and evidence given, do you agree or disagree with the writer's conclusion? Why or why not?

_____

3 Work with a partner. Match each piece of evidence from the chart in Exercise 1 to the type of evidence it is. Write the numbers in the chart.

facts	statistics	expert opinions	quotations	examples	personal experience

4 Work with a partner. Look at the types of evidence in the chart above and the one in Exercise 1. Answer the questions.

1 Which type of evidence was used the most in Reading 2? Why do you think this type was used more than the others?

_____

2 In your experience, which types of evidence are most common in academic writing?

_____

3 Which type of evidence do you find most persuasive? Why?

_____

5 Work with a partner. Brainstorm a list of arguments for and against the statement in the Writing Task.

> The fashion industry is harmful to society and the environment.
> Do you agree or disagree?

6 Work with a partner. Look at your list of arguments in Exercise 5. Decide if you will argue for or against the statement.

7 Write the reasons that support your main argument in the chart. For each reason, think of three or more pieces of evidence to support your position. Try to use a variety of evidence types from the chart above.

main argument: The fashion industry is / is not harmful.		
reason 1: _____	reason 2: _____	reason 3: _____
evidence: _____ _____ _____	evidence: _____ _____ _____	evidence: _____ _____ _____
conclusion: _____		

GRAMMAR FOR WRITING

MULTIWORD PREPOSITIONS

Single-word prepositions like *for* and *with* as well as multiword prepositions like *because of* are followed by nouns, noun phrases, pronouns or gerunds. Some multiword prepositions can be used to join two pieces of information. In the following example, which ideas are connected by the multiword preposition *rather than*?

Critics of outsourcing claim that children should be in full-time education rather than working in a factory.

Common multiword prepositions and their meanings include the following:
Reason: *because of, due to, as a result of*   **Preference:** *rather than, instead of*
Exception: *except for, other than, apart from*   **Concession/contrast:** *in spite of*
Addition: *in addition to, along with*   **Choice:** *instead of*

1 Read the sentences and underline the multiword prepositions. What comes after each preposition—a noun, noun phrase, pronoun or gerund?

1 The low cost of most fast fashion enables shoppers to buy several new sets of clothes each season instead of wearing the same outfits year after year. _____

2 Due to their longer lifespan, expensive designer clothes are more environmentally friendly than cheap clothes. _____

3 Because of the low labor costs in developing nations, multinational companies are able to keep most of the profits from the sale of the clothes produced overseas. _____

4 Conditions in some overseas factories are terrible. In spite of this, many local workers want to get jobs in these factories. _____

5 The United States, along with Europe and Japan, are the leading consumers of fast fashion. _____

2 Replace the underlined prepositions with synonyms from the skills box. Some items have more than one correct answer.

1 The company closed its offshore production facilities <u>along with</u> its overseas retail stores. _____

2 Most people prefer wearing casual clothes <u>rather than</u> formal business suits. _____

3 <u>Except for</u> perfume, I don't use any designer products. _____

4 <u>Because of</u> cheap overseas labor, people in developed countries can buy shirts for five dollars. _____

5 Recently, I started buying some high-end clothes that last <u>instead of</u> fast fashion. _____

3 Complete the sentences with prepositions from the box.

along with	except for	in addition to	in spite of	instead of

1 _____ buying disposable fashion, it is better for the environment if people choose clothes that last longer.

2 _____ encouraging child labor, offshore production also drives wages and working conditions down.

3 _____ the low wages in overseas factories, many people are eager to take these jobs.

4 Workers can't wear any jewelry in the factory _____ wedding rings.

5 Uzbekistan, _____ Brazil, are two countries that export a lot of cotton.

ACADEMIC WRITING SKILLS

BODY PARAGRAPHS IN ARGUMENTATIVE ESSAYS

SKILLS

The introductory paragraph of an argumentative essay describes the issue and includes a statement of the writer's position. The introduction is followed by one or more body paragraphs in which the writer presents arguments that support his or her thesis. The goal of these paragraphs is to convince the reader to agree with the writer's point of view.

Each body paragraph has a topic sentence that presents the writer's supporting argument and reasons and evidence that support the argument.

PRISM Online Workbook

1 Read the thesis statement for a student's essay about the negative effect of the fashion industry on young people's body image. Read the possible topic sentences of the first body paragraph of the essay and choose the one that best supports the thesis statement.

> Thesis statement: *The fashion industry has a negative influence on young people's body image and can cause serious problems, such as depression and eating disorders.*

a Advertising companies use computer enhancement techniques to make photos of models look unrealistically perfect.

b The fashion industry's unrealistic portrayal of the human body can cause young people to become depressed about their looks.

c Pressure from parents to do well in school or get a job can also cause young people to become depressed.

d Rates of depression are especially high among young adults between the ages of 18 and 30.

2 Read the body paragraph of a student's essay below. Circle the topic sentence, where the writer states his or her argument.

Within the fashion industry, some magazines and designers have recently begun promoting a more positive and realistic body image in their products. A leading fashion magazine announced that it would encourage a healthier approach to body image in all its editions. Some fashion companies have begun to use models that have more realistic body types. In addition, Pierre Dupont, a French fashion designer, announced a new collection aimed at celebrating body diversity. "I believe we should represent all body shapes," he said.

3 What evidence does the writer use to support his or her argument in the body paragraph?

_____

_____

4 Work with a partner. Do you think the writer's argument and evidence are convincing? Why or why not?

_____

COHESION

Cohesion refers to the way writers connect ideas in and between sentences. When writing is cohesive, it is clear and easy to follow. Writers use the following techniques to make writing cohesive:

a transitions between sentences or between ideas
b repetition of nouns or use of synonyms
c pronouns that refer back to nouns in earlier sentences
d *this/that/these/those* to refer to earlier nouns or ideas

5 Read the excerpts from Reading 1. Underline and identify the cohesive devices from the box that are being used. The first one is done for you.

PRISM Online Workbook

1 The <u>fashion industry</u> has changed significantly in recent years. Traditionally, fashion retailers created two clothing collections per year, one for each fashion season. Nowadays, in contrast, they can design and manufacture clothes in as little as four weeks.

2 The low cost of most fast fashion enables shoppers to buy several new sets of clothes each season instead of wearing the same outfits year after year. This means that huge amounts of clothing are thrown away. Furthermore, with fashions changing so quickly, cotton growers need to produce more cotton more cheaply, and that means using more pesticides and chemicals.

6 Read the summary of some of the ideas in Readings 1 and 2. Complete the paragraph using the words in the box to make it cohesive.

change	In addition	Meanwhile	ones
that	them	these	they	this	This

The speed of change in the fashion world means that we buy many more clothes than we need. To keep up with (1)_____ fast pace of (2)_____ , retailers create a constant demand for new clothes by selling (3)_____ cheaply and changing items every week. To make space for the new clothes, customers throw away the old (4)_____ as soon as (5)_____ are out of style. (6)_____ way of shopping leads to a higher demand for cotton, and (7)_____ means more intensive agriculture and damage to the environment. (8)_____ , many of (9)_____ cheap clothes are sewn in sweatshops in countries where workers earn less than a dollar a day. (10)_____ , the clothing companies keep nearly all the profits.

WRITING TASK

The fashion industry is harmful to society and the environment. Do you agree or disagree?

PLAN

1 Look at the chart you created in Exercise 7 in Critical Thinking.

2 Use the outline to plan your essay.

Introductory paragraph	• Introduce the topic and give background information about it. • In the thesis statement, state your position and indicate the arguments you will use to support it.
Body paragraphs (2–3)	• Give argument 1 with supporting reasons and evidence. • Give argument 2 with supporting reasons and evidence. • Give argument 3 with supporting reasons and evidence.
Concluding paragraph	• Restate or refer back to your thesis. • Summarize your arguments. • Make a strong final statement to convince your reader to agree with you.

WRITE A FIRST DRAFT

3 Answer the question in the Writing Task by writing an essay with four paragraphs, following your plan in Exercise 2.

REVISE

4 Use the Task Checklist to review your essay for content and structure.

TASK CHECKLIST	✔
Does the introduction include a description of the issue and a thesis statement giving your position?	
In the body paragraphs, did you present arguments to support your position on the topic?	
Did you include reasons and evidence to support each argument?	
In the conclusion, did you repeat your position and summarize your arguments?	
Did you include a strong final statement to persuade the reader to agree with you?	

EDIT

5 Use the Language Checklist to edit your essay for language errors.

LANGUAGE CHECKLIST	✔
Did you use vocabulary for the fashion business?	
Did you use multiword prepositions correctly?	
Did you use cohesive devices to connect your ideas in and between sentences?	

WRITE A FINAL DRAFT

6 Make any necessary changes to your essay.

ON CAMPUS

USING INTERNET SOURCES

The Internet can be a very good resource for finding sources for a paper. It can also be a very bad resource. It is important to know how to evaluate the sources you find there.

PREPARING TO READ

1 Do you use websites as sources for your class assignments? If yes, which of these do you use?

academic journals ☐   nonprofit organization websites ☐
company websites ☐   online newspapers ☐
educational websites ☐   personal blogs ☐
government websites ☐   Wikipedia ☐

○ ● ●

Pederson Library Writing Center   Home   About   **Learn**   Contact

Evaluating Sources on the Internet

When you find sources on the Internet, you must decide if they are reliable sources. You want sources that are written by experts, that are up-to-date, and that are unbiased[1].

Overview of reliable sources

There are certain websites that are usually not reliable sources. In general, you should avoid personal blogs, Wikipedia, and company websites ending in .com. Websites that you can usually trust end in .edu for educational sites and .gov for government sites. Respected newspapers and magazines are also reliable, even though the website ends in .com. Be careful with sites that end in .org or nonprofit sites. Some are reliable, but some are not.

Information to consider when you evaluate[2] a source.

Date: Look for a recent date. In some subject areas, information may not change quickly. However, in some fields, like technology or fashion, trends change quickly, so be sure the information is current. If you can't find a date, it may not be a good source.

Author: You should be able to find the author's name and his or her credentials[3]. Authors should be experts in their field and knowledgeable about the topic. If you are not sure, search for other articles on the topic by that author.

Affiliation[4]: The source should indicate the author's affiliation or connection to a larger organization. It might be the name of a university, a government agency, or a research organization.

Audience: For college-level work, the source material should be written for college-level readers, not for high school or younger readers.

[1]**unbiased** (adj) fair and not influenced by personal opinions
[2]**evaluate** (v) judge or decide if something is useful
[3]**credentials** (n) proof of someone's ability and experience
[4]**affiliation** (n) a connection to a larger organization

WHILE READING

2 Read the page from a website about how to choose the most reliable websites and match the situation with the advice according to the reading.

1 You find a website that ends in .org. _____
2 You don't know if the author is an expert. _____
3 You find an article about fitness trackers with no date. _____
4 You find a blog by a woman who goes to fitness centers and writes about her experience. _____
5 You find a high school website called Health for Today. _____

a Don't use the article because it may not be current.
b Don't use something that is for younger readers.
c Do a search to find other articles by that person.
d Don't use the article because it is mostly personal opinion.
e Do more research to find out about the organization.

PRACTICE

3 Work with a partner. Look at a student's notes for three sources about teen health. Discuss how reliable these sources are and why.

1 Junk Food in Schools and Child Obesity, National Institutes of Health
Website: http://www.ncbi.nlm.nih.gov
Author: A.Datar and N. Nicosia
Date: Spring 2012
Affiliation: National Center for Biotechnology Information

2 The New Face of Hunger, National Geographic Magazine
Website: http://www.nationalgeographic.com
Author: Tracie McMillan
Date: None given
Affiliation: Schuster Institute for Investigative Journalism

3 Healthier Schools Meals, Time for Kids
Website: http://www.timeforkids.com
Author: Suraj Modi
Date: September 23, 2015
Affiliation: None given

REAL-WORLD APPLICATION

4 Work with a partner. Imagine you are writing a paper on how parents can help teens make healthy choices.

1 Search for Internet sources about the topic, "healthy choices for teens."
2 Choose two websites and decide if they are reliable sources.

5 Share your results and decision with another team.

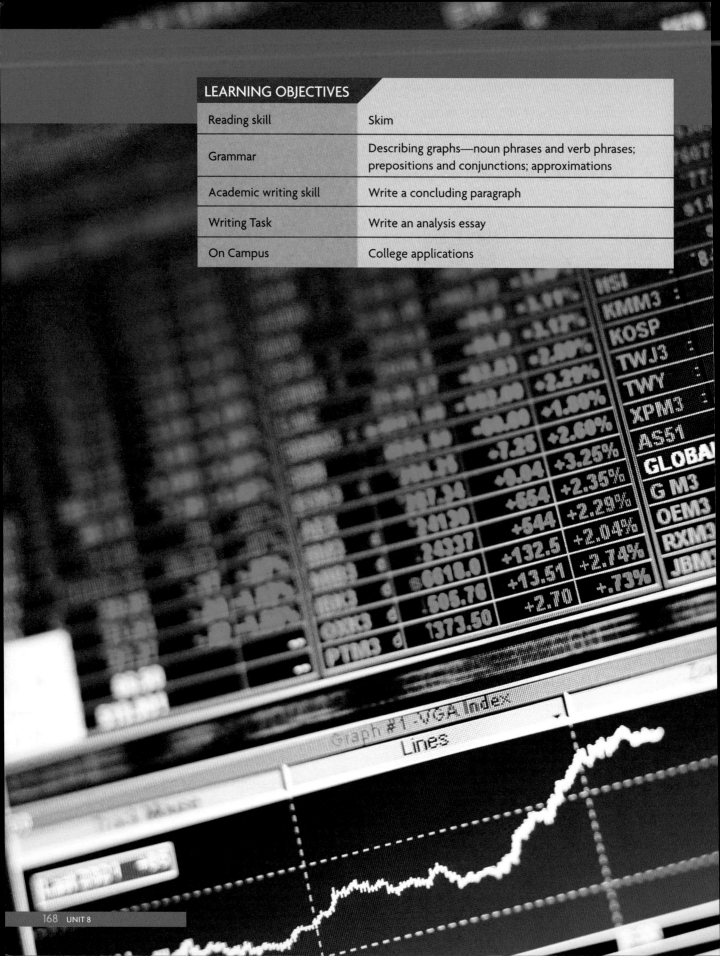

LEARNING OBJECTIVES

Reading skill	Skim
Grammar	Describing graphs—noun phrases and verb phrases; prepositions and conjunctions; approximations
Academic writing skill	Write a concluding paragraph
Writing Task	Write an analysis essay
On Campus	College applications

ACTIVATE YOUR KNOWLEDGE

Work with a partner. Discuss the questions.

1 Do you believe it is important for people to be informed about economics? Why or why not?
2 What causes some countries to be rich and other countries to be poor?
3 How has the economy of your country changed in recent years?

PREPARING TO WATCH

1 Work with a partner. Discuss the questions.

1 What cities in the world today are centers of finance?
2 What happens during an economic depression?
3 How healthy is the economy of your country?

2 You are going to watch a video about a very bad day for the world economy. Before you watch, work with a partner and use the photos from the video and your own knowledge to answer the questions.

1 Where did it happen?
2 When did it happen?
3 How did it happen?
4 Who did it affect?

GLOSSARY

stock market (n) a system for buying and selling stocks; the total value of all the investments that are traded in this system

crash (v) to fall or lose value suddenly and completely

investor (n) someone who puts money in a bank, business, etc. in order to make a profit

depression (n) a period in which there is very little business activity and little employment

replica (n) a copy of an object

ticker tape (n) a long, thin strip of paper, used in the past for printing changing information on, for example, the prices of stocks

---

WHILE WATCHING

3 ▶ Watch the video. Check your answers to Exercise 2.

4 ▶ Watch the video again. Match the sentence halves.

1 The stock market _____
2 On Black Tuesday, investors _____
3 Millions of people _____
4 The Great Depression _____
5 Ticker tape machines _____

a was the worst economic period in modern history.
b were used to print the prices of stocks and shares.
c crashed in 1929.
d lost their jobs.
e lost billions of dollars.

UNDERSTANDING MAIN IDEAS

5 ▶ Watch the video again. Answer the questions.

1 When did Black Tuesday happen? _____
2 Who was affected by the crash? _____
3 What happened to stock prices after Black Tuesday?

_____
4 Where is the Museum of Financial History? _____
5 What does the stock exchange use now to report stock prices?

_____

UNDERSTANDING DETAILS

6 Work with a partner. Discuss the questions and give reasons for your answers.

1 Were most financial experts surprised by Black Tuesday?
2 Why did people in other countries lose their jobs during the Depression?
3 How have computers changed stock markets?

MAKING INFERENCES

DISCUSSION

7 Work in a small group. Discuss your answers.

1 What are the biggest economic problems in the world today?
2 How do changes in the economy affect your daily life?
3 Do you think the economy will be better in ten years? Why or why not?

READING

PREPARING TO READ

UNDERSTANDING
KEY VOCABULARY

1 You are going to read an article about investments. Read the sentences. Complete the definitions with the correct form of the words in bold.

1 During the **recession** of 2007–2009, people all over the world lost their jobs and were forced to sell their homes.
2 At my bank, the **interest rate** on a loan to buy a car is about 4.5%.
3 Since Apple Computer company **stocks and shares** went on sale in 1976, their value has increased by more than 28,000%.
4 Real estate, that is, land or buildings, is an excellent **investment** in large cities like Los Angeles or Tokyo.
5 My father is a careful **investor**. He buys assets, like buildings and cars, that increase slowly but surely over time.
6 After a natural disaster such as a tsunami or fire, the homes and businesses in an area usually go down in **value**.
7 If you buy gold, you can probably expect to get a high rate of **return** on your investment.

a _____ (n) the percentage amount that you pay when you borrow money, or receive when you lend money, for a period of time
b _____ (n) profit on an investment
c _____ (n) parts of a publicly owned business that can be bought and sold as investments
d _____ (n) someone who puts money in a bank, business, etc. to make a profit
e _____ (n) how much money something could be sold for
f _____ (n) a period when the economy of a country is not doing well, but not as bad as a depression
g _____ (n) something such as stocks, bonds, or property that you buy in order to make a profit

USING YOUR
KNOWLEDGE

2 Work with a partner. Discuss the questions.

1 If people want to make money, what can they invest in?
2 What is the safest investment, in your opinion?
3 Do you think it is better to invest in gold or in classic cars?

How should you invest your money?

1   In a **recession**, **interest rates** are low. This means that keeping your money in a bank may not be the best way of making money. **Stocks and shares** are also risky when the economy takes a dive[1]. So where should you invest to make the most of your money? For the brave **investor**, there are a range of alternative **investments**. Gold and classic cars are two popular investments because their market **value** tends to go up with time.

2   Over time, gold has been a very good investment, though the price has fluctuated[2] in recent years, as the graph below shows. From about $283 an ounce at the turn of the 21st century, the price had more than doubled by 2006 and then doubled again, to $1,224, by 2010. Continuing the upward trend, the price rose sharply in 2011 and then reached a peak of $1,800 an ounce in 2012. However, by the end of 2015 the price had fallen dramatically, to $1,160. Forecasters expect the price to stay in this range through 2020, so if you are thinking about investing in gold, you may want to consider one famous investor's advice. Warren Buffet, one of the richest men in the world, dislikes gold as an investment. He points out that historically, the stock market has brought in significantly higher **returns** than gold. This is not always true, however. Between 2000 and 2012, for example, gold performed nearly ten times better than the stock market.

3   While gold and stocks are both excellent investment options, some people prefer investments that they can use and enjoy. For these people, classic cars are one way to have fun and make lots of money. In fact, over the last 30 or 40 years, the value of some classic cars has risen far more than that of gold or other investments like houses. As an example, a 1972 Ferrari Dino 246 GT cost around $13,000 in 1980 but is worth as much as $450,000 now. A 1955 Mercedes Benz 300SL cost about $36,000 in 1980 but is worth more than $1 million now. But neither of these cars compares to what is perhaps the best investment ever: A man in Tennessee bought the Aston Martin DB5 that was used in two of the James Bond films. This car cost just $7,000 in 1980 but sold in 2010 for an incredible $4.1 million! That is more than 20 times the price of an average American home!

4   In sum, the prospect of making lots of money through investing is very exciting, but one must never forget that investing is a risky business. Gold prices rise, but they also fall. Classic cars need to be kept in excellent condition to increase in value and, because fashions change, investors have to guess which car to invest in. If you are smart and lucky, you may make a big profit—but remember, there are no guarantees.

[1]**take a dive** (v) If a value or price takes a dives, it suddenly becomes less.
[2]**fluctuate** (v) to keep changing, especially in level or amount

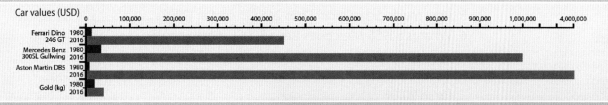

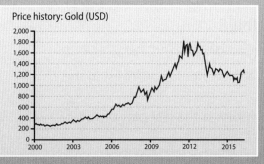

WHILE READING

SKIMMING

PRISM Online Workbook

READING FOR MAIN IDEAS

READING FOR DETAILS

MAKING INFERENCES

3 Skim the article and the graphs. Check the topics that the article discusses.

causes of a recession ☐   the stock market in 2016 ☐
two popular investments ☐   classic cars as an investment ☐
the price of gold over time ☐ the risks of investing ☐

4 Look at your answers to Exercise 3. Find the main ideas and write them in the order that they appear in the reading.

Paragraph 1 _____
Paragraph 2 _____
Paragraph 3 _____
Paragraph 4 _____

5 Read the article again. Answer the questions using a figure from the article. Remember that you can annotate the text as you read.

1 Approximately how much did gold cost per ounce at the beginning of the 21st century? _____
2 What happened to the price of gold in 2006? _____
3 In which year was the price of gold the highest? How much did it cost per ounce? _____
4 According to forecasters, what will happen to the price of gold between now and 2020? _____
5 How much did a Ferrari Dino 246 GT cost in 1980? _____
6 What is a 1955 Mercedes Benz 300SL worth now?

   _____

7 How much did the Aston Martin used in the James Bond films sell for in 2010? _____

READING BETWEEN THE LINES

6 Work with a partner. Discuss the questions.

1 If you followed Warren Buffet's advice, would you invest in the stock market or in gold? Why?
2 Which investment had a better return in the first part of the 21st century: gold or a classic car?
3 Are classic cars a risky investment? Why or why not?

DISCUSSION

7 Work with a partner. Discuss the questions.

1 Imagine that you and your partner have one million dollars to invest. How would you invest the money? Why?

2 Are there any investments that you definitely would not make? Why would you choose not to invest your money in this way?

3 If you could afford it, would you buy an Aston Martin DB5? Why or why not?

READING 2

PREPARING TO READ

1 You are going to read an article about income and expenditure. Before you read the article, read the sentences below. Complete the definitions with the correct form of the words in bold.

UNDERSTANDING
KEY VOCABULARY

PRISM Online Workbook

1 My family has a comfortable **standard of living**. We have enough money to pay for everything we need, and we are able to save a little bit of money every month.

2 People who go to college usually have a higher **income** than people with only a high-school diploma.

3 Housing is the biggest **expenditure** for most people. Many Americans pay nearly 40% of their income in rent or house payments.

4 The weather is one **factor** that influences the price of food. For example, if there is not enough rain, crops are smaller and the price of food goes up.

5 Families with many children must spend a large **percentage** of their income on food and clothing.

6 It is a smart idea for workers to put some money into **savings** every month. Even $20 a month can grow into a large amount over time.

a _____ (n) money that you put away, usually in a bank, for a later date

b _____ (n) how much money and comfort someone has

c _____ (n) one of the things that has an effect on a particular situation, decision, event, etc.

d _____ (n) the total amount of money that a government or person spends on something

e _____ (n) money that you earn by working, investing, or producing goods

f _____ (n) an amount of something, expressed as a number out of 100

2 Work with a partner. Answer the questions.

1 Do you think the standard of living in the United States has improved, gotten worse, or stayed the same in the last 20 years?

_____

2 What factor or factors play an important role in determining people's standard of living? _____

3 Scan the article and check your answers.

WHILE READING

4 Read and annotate the article opposite. Look at page 85 for what to annotate.

5 Choose the sentence that is the best summary of the article.

a The article compares income and expenditure in the United States with the same factors in other developed countries.

b The article explains how falling incomes and rising expenditure has affected Americans' standard of living in recent years.

c The article describes five categories of expenditure that play a key role in determining people's standard of living.

d The article discusses how the American Dream became a reality for Americans in the years during and following the Second World War.

6 Read the article again and choose the correct statement from each pair.

1 a Incomes rose quickly from 1995 to 2000, but they have been increasing very slowly since then.

b Incomes rose quickly from 1995 to 2000 but they have been decreasing since then.

2 a Between 1999 and 2014, median income fell by about 7%.

b Since 1999, median income in the U.S. has risen by about $4,000.00.

3 a Between 1996 and 2014, Americans spent more on transportation than they did on food.

b Between 1996 and 2014, Americans' biggest expenditure was housing.

4 a Healthcare costs have stayed approximately the same in spite of rising hospital costs.

b Because of higher prices for prescription drugs and hospital stays, healthcare costs have increased by about 100%.

5 a To meet their monthly expenditure, many Americans are using savings or borrowing money.

b To meet their monthly expenditure, many Americans are investing more money in real estate or the stock market.

1   One common definition of the "American Dream" is the belief that each generation will do better than the one before it. Unfortunately, many Americans today are not able to enjoy the same **standard of living** as their parents before them. The reason is that for the past 20 years, **incomes** have been declining while **expenditure** has been rising. In effect, this means many people are actually poorer than they were 20 years ago.

2   Falling incomes are the first cause of the declining standard of living. From 1945 to 1973, incomes increased by approximately 3% per year. From the mid-1970s to the mid-1990s, they continued to rise, though more slowly; but then they increased sharply between 1995 and 2000. Since 2000, however, incomes have been falling steadily. According to the U.S. Census Bureau, the median income was $57,724 in 1999 and just $53,657 in 2014.

3   The other key **factor** in determining people's standard of living is expenditure. Figure 1 shows the **percentage** of their income that Americans spent on five key categories between 1996 and 2014: housing; food; transportation; pets, toys, and entertainment; and health. Until 2013, the costs for these five categories remained more or less stable. That is, Americans spent approximately 20% of their incomes on housing, about 10% on food, about 8%

on transportation, and around 3% each for pets, toys, and entertainment, and health. As the graph shows clearly, except for pets, toys, and entertainment, all these costs jumped in 2013. By 2014, for instance, Americans were spending 25% of their income for housing and about 12% for food.

4   There are many reasons for rising expenditure over time, but two important ones are the high cost of housing and healthcare. In many cities, there is a critical shortage of houses and apartments to buy and rent. This has driven up costs. Also, healthcare costs have doubled since 1996 as prescription drugs and hospital costs have gotten more and more expensive. Transportation and food prices have also increased significantly in recent years.

5   In conclusion, the combination of rising prices and falling incomes has left many Americans with less spending power than they had 20 years ago. Because people must pay more for essentials like housing and food, they have less money for education, investment, savings, and small luxuries like eating in restaurants. Many people have had to sell their homes, use up their **savings**, or borrow money in order to meet their monthly expenditure. For these people, the American Dream must seem very far out of reach. Sadly, no one seems to know how or when the situation will improve.

[1]**median** (adj) having a value that is exactly in the middle of a set of values arranged from largest to smallest

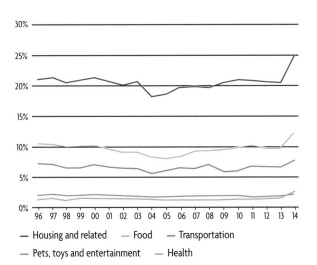

— Housing and related   — Food   — Transportation

— Pets, toys and entertainment   — Health

READING BETWEEN THE LINES

MAKING INFERENCES

7 Work with a partner. Answer the questions.

1 In the graph on page 177, why are pets, toys, and entertainment combined into one group?

____

2 What could have caused the price of transportation to increase between 1996 and 2014?

____

3 If the average person earned around $53,600 in 2014, about how much did that person spend on housing?

____

DISCUSSION

SYNTHESIZING

8 Work with a partner. Use ideas from Reading 1 and Reading 2 to answer the following questions.

1 Do most Americans probably have more, less, or about the same amount of money to invest as they did 20 years ago? Why?
2 If someone's income is falling and expenditure is rising, is it a good idea to try to make more money by investing in the stock market, gold, etc.? Why or why not?
3 What has happened to income and expenditure in your country since 1996? Why?

LANGUAGE DEVELOPMENT

NOUNS AND ADJECTIVES FOR ECONOMICS

PRISM Online Workbook

1 Use a dictionary to find the meanings of the words in the chart.

noun	adjective
1 economy	economic
2 finance	financial
3 wealth	wealthy
4 poverty	poor
5 value	valuable
6 employment	employed
7 profession	professional
8 expense	expensive

2 Complete the sentences using either an adjective or a noun from the chart in Exercise 1 on the opposite page.

1 Since 1999 the U.S. _____ has been weak, with little growth.
2 Companies that are losing money often turn to the banks for _____ assistance.
3 Only _____ investors can afford to buy expensive classic cars.
4 As incomes have fallen in recent years, more and more Americans have fallen into _____ .
5 Many wealthy people enjoy spending their money to buy _____ art.
6 Each month, the U.S. government publishes the latest _____ statistics on how many people are in work.
7 _____ services like legal or financial advice can cost a lot of money.
8 It is _____ to buy even a single share in some successful companies, so you might want to start with companies whose shares cost a few dollars each.

NOUNS FOR ECONOMIC TRENDS

3 Read the definitions. Complete the sentences with the correct form of the words in bold.

> **consumer** (n) a person who buys a product or service to use
> **demand** (n) the need for something to be sold or supplied
> **market** (n) the total number of people who might want to buy something
> **purchase** (n) something that you buy
> **revenue** (n) the income that a company or government receives
> **supply** (n) an amount or quantity of something available to use
> **trend** (n) the general direction of trends and developments

1 The _____ for fast fashion is enormous in developed countries such as the United States, United Kingdom, and Japan.
2 I was not satisfied with my _____ , so I returned the item to the store.
3 When shopping for large items like cars and refrigerators, smart _____ compare prices before they make their decision.
4 A recent fashion _____ for women is shoes with extremely high heels.
5 The company failed because there was not enough _____ for the service it was selling.
6 _____ from movie downloads has increased by more than 200% since 2010.
7 Prices go up when there is not enough _____ of a product or service that people want.

WRITING

CRITICAL THINKING

At the end of this unit, you will write an analysis essay about a graph. Look at this unit's Writing Task in the box below.

> ▶ Describe the multiple-line graph showing home video revenue and explain the data.

Understanding line graphs

A line graph uses points on a line to show a trend. Use the following strategies to read and understand a line graph:

- Read the title. It gives the subject of the graph and often summarizes the most important trend that the data show.
- The time period covered by the graph normally appears on the horizontal axis of the graph, that is, the line that goes from left to right along the bottom. Is it in years, months, weeks, or days?
- Now look at the vertical axis—the line that goes from top to bottom on the left side of the graph. This axis shows numbers or percentages.
- To "read" a line graph, notice the points where the vertical axis and horizontal axis meet. Each point tells you the number or percentage that matches one of the years along the bottom of the graph.
- Many line graphs have more than one line. In this way, one graph can show more than one trend. Each line will have a different color or pattern. Look for the *legend*—the box or sentence that explains what each color or pattern means.

▲ UNDERSTAND

1 Work with a partner. Look at the graph from Reading 2 on page 177. Answer the questions to help you read and understand the graph.

1 What trend or "main idea" does the graph show?

_____

2 What is the meaning of the numbers on the left side of the graph?

_____

3 Which years are covered by the graph? _____

4 Why does the graph have 5 lines in different colors? What does each color mean? _____

5 What percentage of their income did Americans spend on food in 1998? _____

6 From 1996 to 2004, did the percentage of income that Americans spent on transportation increase or decrease? _____

7 What trend do you see starting in 2004? Is it the same for all five types of expenditure? _____

Interpreting a line graph

Once you have understood the information in a line graph, you need to interpret it. This means identifying relationships between the points on the graph and trying to explain any trends that emerge from the data. (Note: Graphs contain facts, not reasons. You will need to use your own information or do research in order to interpret the data.) If the graph has more than one line, you also need to identify the relationships between the sets of data.

2 Work with a partner. Look at the graph again and answer the questions.

ANALYZE

1 What general trends do the data show between 1996 and 2004 and between 2004 and 2014? How do you explain these trends?

_____
_____
_____
_____
_____
_____

2 Between 1996 and 2014, which of the five types of expenditure went up and down most often? Why do you think this expenditure changed more than any of the others?

_____
_____
_____

3 Which expenditure did not change between 1996 and 2013? Why?

_____
_____

4 What happened in 2013? Do you think this change was caused by a particular event, or is it normal for expenditure to change this way from time to time?

_____
_____

5 Based on the information in the graph, what can you conclude about Americans' standard of living in 2014?

_____

3 Work with a partner. Look at the graph. Answer the questions to help you read and understand the graph.

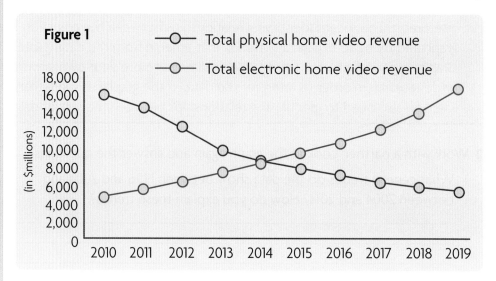

Figure 1

—○— Total physical home video revenue

—○— Total electronic home video revenue

1 The graph compares "physical" and "electronic" home video revenue. What do these terms mean? Which line on the graph represents which term?

_____

_____

2 Which years are covered? _____

3 What is the meaning of the numbers on the vertical axis?

_____

4 In what year did sales of physical home videos equal sales of electronic home videos? _____

4 Complete the summary with figures from the graph.

In 2010, sales from physical home videos were worth about $ (1)_____ m, compared to only about $ (2)_____ m for electronic home videos. Revenues from these two types of home video are expected to be exactly the opposite by the year (3)_____ .

5 Answer the following questions to help you interpret the graph.

1 Summarize the trend shown in the graph. Complete this sentence: According to the figure, revenues from physical home video sales and electronic home video sales have moved in opposite directions. As revenue from sales of (1)_____ has risen, revenue from sales of (2)_____ has fallen.

2 What reason or reasons can you think of to explain the trend in Question 1?

_____

_____

DESCRIBING GRAPHS—NOUN PHRASES AND VERB PHRASES

LANGUAGE

You can describe data with a verb phrase (a verb + an adverb) or a noun phrase (an article + an adjective + a noun).

Verb phrase
Sales of DVDs **rose sharply** and then **decreased sharply**.

Noun phrase
There was **a sharp rise** in sales of DVDs and then **a sharp decrease**.

1 Match the sentences to the graphs.

PRISM Online Workbook

1 Sales of DVDs rose sharply and then fell dramatically. _____
2 DVD sales decreased slightly and then decreased sharply. _____
3 The number of DVD sales did not change. _____
4 Television sales increased slightly and then increased sharply. _____
5 At first, the number of DVDs sold did not change, but later this figure fluctuated. _____
6 DVD sales fell slightly but did not change after that. _____

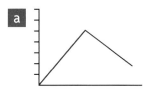

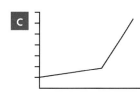
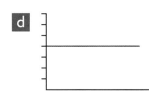
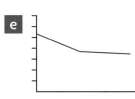
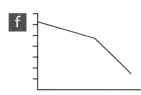

2 Write the verb phrases as noun phrases.

1 rise sharply   *a sharp rise*
2 fall dramatically   _____
3 decrease slightly   _____
4 increase gradually   _____
5 fluctuate considerably   _____

PREPOSITIONS AND CONJUNCTIONS

You can use prepositions and conjunctions to add data.

Sales increased sharply **from** 7.68 **to** 10.63 million units **between** 2003 **and** 2004.

You can use *of* in a noun phrase to describe the total change.

This was an increase **of** 2.95 million units.

PRISM Online Workbook

3 Complete the sentences using the words in bold in the examples above.

1 Sales fell _____ 1.1 million _____ 1 million units, a decrease _____ 100,000 units.

2 Prices rose _____ around $5.00 _____ well over $10.00—a rise _____ 100%.

3 _____ 2008 _____ 2009, prices decreased slightly, _____ $7.75 _____ $7.00.

4 Prices fluctuated considerably _____ 2010 _____ 2011.

5 There was a gradual increase in prices _____ $8.00 _____ $8.95 during the last six months of the year.

APPROXIMATIONS

PRISM Online Workbook

4 Fill in the blanks with words and phrases from the box that have the same meaning as the first word in each row.

about	approximately	around	nearly	over	under

1 almost _____

2 more than _____

3 roughly _____ _____ _____

4 less than _____

5 Match the phrases to the figures.

1	almost a hundred dollars	a	$11,156
2	roughly a thousand dollars	b	$485,134
3	over ten thousand dollars	c	$240,000
4	more than eleven thousand dollars	d	$1,014
5	less than a quarter of a million dollars	e	$10,237
6	roughly half a million dollars	f	$996,001
7	approximately a million dollars	g	$99.99

ACADEMIC WRITING SKILLS

WRITING A CONCLUDING PARAGRAPH

The concluding paragraph of an academic essay should end the essay without adding any new main ideas. It should be shorter than the body of the essay. Typically, this paragraph has three parts:

- **a transition phrase.** Common phrases include *in conclusion, in short, in summary, to summarize, to sum up*, or *to conclude*.
- **a restatement or repetition of the thesis statement from the introduction.** Strategies for restating include changing the order of phrases and clauses, and using different words for the same concepts or ideas. For words that do not have synonyms, it is fine to repeat them in your conclusion.
- **a final comment.** This is your final message to your reader. It can be your opinion, a prediction about the future, a recommendation, a call to action on the part of the reader, or a combination of these. If you are writing about a graph, it is common to conclude by stating the possible effects or implications of the data.

1 Read the thesis statement and last paragraph of Reading 2 below. Then:

PRISM Online Workbook

1 Underline the sentence in the concluding paragraph that restates the thesis.
2 Circle the transition phrase in the concluding paragraph.
3 Put a box around the final comments in the concluding paragraph. Which of the following does the writer include? Choose more than one.
   a an opinion
   b a prediction about the future
   c a recommendation
   d the implications of the data in the graph

Thesis statement
... for the past 20 years, incomes have been declining while expenditure has been rising. In effect, this means many people are actually poorer than they were 20 years ago.

Concluding paragraph
In conclusion, the combination of rising prices and falling incomes has left many Americans with less spending power than they had 20 years ago. Because people must pay more for essentials like housing and food, they have less money for education, investment, savings, and small luxuries like eating in restaurants. Many people have had to sell their homes, use up their savings, or borrow money in order to meet their monthly expenditure. For these people, the American Dream must seem very far out of reach. Sadly, no one seems to know how or when the situation will improve.

WRITING TASK

Describe the multiple-line graph showing home video revenue and explain the data.

PLAN

1 Look at the questions you answered in Exercises 3–5 of Critical Thinking.

2 Plan your introductory paragraph. Write notes for the hook, background information, and thesis statement of your introduction.

3 Outline the body of your essay. It should have two paragraphs. You should describe the graph in the first paragraph. You should interpret the data in the second paragraph.

4 Plan your concluding paragraph. It should restate your thesis statement and include final remarks.

_____

_____

5 Use the Task Checklist below as you prepare your essay.

WRITE A FIRST DRAFT

6 Write the first draft of your essay using your essay plan.

REVISE

7 Use the Task Checklist to review your essay for content and structure.

TASK CHECKLIST	✔
Does your introduction include a hook, background information and a thesis statement?	
Did you write two body paragraphs, one describing the graph and one interpreting the graph?	
Did you refer to the graph in the body paragraphs?	
Did you write a concluding paragraph that restates the thesis and includes final remarks?	

EDIT

8 Use the Language Checklist to edit your essay for language errors.

LANGUAGE CHECKLIST	✔
Did you use nouns and adjectives for economics (e.g., *finance, financial*)?	
Did you use nouns for economic trends e.g., (*trend, consumer, market*)?	
Did you vary your language, using noun phrases, verb phrases, and synonyms to describe graphs?	
Did you use prepositions and conjunctions (e.g., *from, to, between, and, of*) to add data?	
Did you use words and phrases for approximations (*more than, under, around, roughly,* etc.)?	

WRITE A FINAL DRAFT

9 Make any necessary changes to your paragraphs.

COLLEGE APPLICATIONS

PREPARING TO READ

1 You are going to read student comments about the college application process. Before you read, work with a partner and answer the questions.

  1 What tasks do you need to complete to apply for a college or university in the United States?
  2 If you needed letters of reference to apply to college, who would you ask? Why?
  3 How do you think the application process in the United States is different from the process in your country?

💬 **Subject:** *College Applications!*   👤👤👤👤 **Chatroom 1:** 4 People

Ahmed

The application process has a lot of steps. I thought I could do it in about a month, but it takes almost a year. At first it seemed like too much, but I made this checklist of all the steps and it helped.

- Take SAT: January 6
- Take IELTS exam: March 14
- Send test scores deadline: May 31
- Order transcript[1] from high school
- Get transcript translated
- Request letters of recommendation
- Write personal statement
- Application deadline: December 1

Margaux

The hardest thing was the personal statement[2]. I was told to be honest and even creative. I wanted to write about my academic record and awards, but a counselor told me I should write something that shows my personality.

Li Wei

In my country, the college admission[3] test score is everything. Here, things like volunteering, work experience, or extracurricular activities are also really important. They even consider things like personal challenges that a student has faced. They're interested in the whole person, not just high school grades and test scores.

Zeyneb

I applied to a Master's Program in microbiology, and I needed two letters of recommendation[5]. I asked my English teacher, but she told me it would be better if I chose a professor in my field because he knows my academic ability. I work at a lab, so I also asked my supervisor.

[1]**transcript** (n) a list of courses and grades for a student

[2]**personal statement** (n) an essay written by a student for a college application

[3]**admission** (n) permission to study at a college or university

[4]**extracurricular** (adj) not part of a school or college program

[5]**letter of recommendation** (n) a letter that describes someone's qualities and abilities

WHILE READING

2 Read the students' comments and write *T* (true), *F* (false) or *DNS* (does not say) next to the statements.

_____ **1** The deadline for test scores is not the same as the application deadline.

_____ **2** It takes about 3 months to find out if you are admitted to a college or university.

_____ **3** It's OK to be creative in a personal statement because it shows your personality.

_____ **4** If a transcript is not in English, the college will translate it.

PRACTICE

3 Complete the pre-application worksheet with information about yourself.

Program: graduate ☐   undergraduate ☐
Academic interests and goals: _____
Academic strengths: _____
Previous extracurricular activities: _____

English Proficiency Exams
TOEFL Date planned/taken: _____   Scores: _____
IELTS Date planned/taken: _____   Scores: _____

College Admissions
SAT Date planned/taken: _____   Scores: _____
GRE Date planned/taken: _____   Scores: _____

Transcripts
Name of school: _____   Date requested: _____

Letters of recommendation
Name: _____   Role: _____
Date to contact: _____
Name: _____   Role: _____
Date to contact: _____

REAL-WORLD APPLICATION

4 Visit the admissions page of a website for a college or university you want to apply to.

1 Answer the questions.
   a What are the key dates and deadlines?
   b Which exams are required?
   c Are letters of recommendation required? How many?
   d What is required for the personal statement?
2 Make a checklist of the things you need to do to apply.

5 Share your checklist with a partner.

GLOSSARY OF KEY VOCABULARY

Words that are part of the Academic Word List are noted with an **Ⓐ** in this glossary.

UNIT 1 ANIMALS

READING 1

chemical Ⓐ (n) man-made or natural substance made by changing atoms

destroy (v) to damage something very badly; to cause it to not exist

due to (prep) because of; as a result of

endangered (adj) (of plants and animals) that may disappear soon

natural (adj) as found in nature; not made or caused by people

pollute (v) to make an area or substance dirty and unhealthful

protect (v) to keep something or someone safe from damage or injury

species (n) types of plants or animals that have similar features

READING 2

common (adj) happening often or existing in large numbers

cruel (adj) causing pain or suffering on purpose

disease (n) illness; a serious health condition that requires care

fatal (adj) causing death

major Ⓐ (adj) most serious or important

native (adj) used to describe animals and plants that grow naturally in a place

survive Ⓐ (v) to continue to live after almost dying

UNIT 2 THE ENVIRONMENT

READING 1

atmosphere (n) the layer of air and gases around the Earth

cause (n) someone or something that makes something happen

climate (n) the general weather conditions usually found in a particular place

ecosystem (n) all the living things in an area and the effect they have on each other and the environment

fossil fuel (n) a source of energy like coal, gas, and petroleum, that was formed inside the Earth millions of years ago

global warming (n) an increase in the Earth's temperature because of pollution

greenhouse gas (n) a gas that makes the air around the Earth warmer

threaten (v) to be likely to damage or harm something

READING 2

absorb (v) to take in a liquid or gas, through a surface and hold it

construction Ⓐ (n) the process of building something, usually large structures such as houses, roads, or bridges

destruction (n) the act of causing so much damage to something that it stops existing because it cannot be repaired

effect (n) result; a change that happens because of a cause

farming (n) the job of working on a farm or organizing work on a farm

logging (n) the activity or business of cutting down trees for wood

rainforest (n) a forest in a tropical area that gets a lot of rain

UNIT 3 TRANSPORTATION

READING 1

commuter (n) someone who travels between home and work or school regularly

connect (v) to join two things or places together

destination (n) the place where someone or something is going

outskirts (n) the outer area of a city or town

public transportation (n) a system of vehicles, such as buses and subways, which operate at regular times for public use

rail (adj) trains as a method of transportation

traffic congestion (n) when too many vehicles use a road network and it results in slower speeds or no movement at all

READING 2

cycle (v) to travel by bicycle

emergency (n) an unexpected situation that requires immediate action

engineering (n) the activity of designing and building things like bridges, roads, machines, etc.

fuel (n) a substance like gas or coal that produces energy when it is burned

government (n) the group of people that controls a country or city and makes decisions about laws, taxes, education, etc.

practical (adj) useful; suitable for the situation it is being used for

vehicle (A) (n) any machine that travels on roads, such as cars, buses, etc.

UNIT 4 CUSTOMS AND TRADITIONS

READING 1

appearance (n) the way someone or something looks

culture (A) (n) a society with its own ideas, traditions, and ways of behaving

exchange (v) to give something to someone, and receive something that they give you

expect (v) to think that something will or should happen

formal (adj) correct or conservative in style, dress, or speech; not casual

greet (v) to welcome someone with particular words or actions

relationship (n) the way two people or groups feel and behave toward each other

READING 2

belief (n) an idea that you are certain is true

ceremony (n) a formal event with special traditions, activities, or words, such as a wedding

couple (A) (n) two people who are married or in a relationship

engaged (adj) having a formal agreement to get married

reception (n) a formal party that is given to celebrate a special event or to welcome someone

relative (n) any member of your family

theme (A) (n) the main idea, subject, or topic of an event, book, musical piece, etc.

UNIT 5 HEALTH AND FITNESS

READING 1

active (adj) doing things that involve movement and energy

calorie (n) measurement of the amount of energy found in food

moderate (adj) not too much and not too little

recognize (v) to understand; to accept that something is true

reduce (v) to limit; to use less of something

self-esteem (n) a feeling of confidence and pride in yourself

serious (adj) bad or dangerous

READING 2

balanced diet (n) a daily eating program that has a healthy mixture of different kinds of food

campaign (n) a group of activities designed to motivate people to take action, such as giving money or changing their behavior

junk food (n) food that is unhealthy but quick and easy to eat

nutritional (adj) relating to food and the way it affects your health

obesity (n) the condition of being extremely overweight

portion Ⓐ (n) an amount of food served to one person

UNIT 6 DISCOVERY AND INVENTION

READING 1

essential (adj) very important or necessary

harmful (adj) able to hurt or damage

helpful (adj) useful

illustrate Ⓐ (v) to show the meaning or truth of something more clearly, especially by giving examples

pattern (n) a set of lines, colors, or shapes that repeat in a regular way

prevent (v) to stop something from happening or stop someone from doing something

unlimited (adj) without end or restriction

READING 2

artificial (adj) not natural; made by people

break down (phr v) to stop working

electronic (adj) sent or accessed by means of a computer or other electronic device

movement (n) a change of position or place

object (n) a thing you can see or touch that isn't alive

personal (adj) belonging or used by just one person

power (n) energy, usually electricity, used to provide heat, light, etc.

three-dimensional (adj) not flat; having depth, length, and width

UNIT 7 FASHION

READING 1

brand (n) the name of a product or group of products made by a company

collection (n) a group of new clothes produced by a fashion house

cotton (n) a plant with white fibers used for making cloth

invest Ⓐ (v) to use money for the purpose of making a profit, for example, by building a factory

manufacture (v) to make goods in a large quantity in a factory

season (n) a time of year when particular things happen

volume Ⓐ (n) amount of something, especially when it is large

READING 2

conditions (n) the physical environment where people live or work

import (v) to buy a product from another country and bring it into your country

multinational (adj) referring to a business or company that has offices, stores, or factories in several countries

offshore (adj) located in another country

outsource (v) to have work done by another company, often in another country, rather than in your own company

textile (n) cloth or fabric that is made by crossing threads under and over each other

wage (n) money that people earn for working

UNIT 8 ECONOMICS

READING 1

interest rate (n) the percentage amount that you pay when you borrow money, or receive when you lend money, for a period of time

investment Ⓐ (n) something such as stocks, bonds, or property that you buy in order to make a profit

investor Ⓐ (n) someone who puts money in a bank, business, etc. to make a profit

recession (n) a period when the economy of a country is not doing well

return (n) profit on an investment

stocks and shares (n) parts of a publicly owned business that can be bought and sold

value (n) how much money something could be sold for

READING 2

expenditure (n) the total amount of money that a government or person spends on something

factor Ⓐ (n) one of the things that has an effect on a particular situation, decision, event, etc.

income Ⓐ (n) money that you earn by working, investing, or producing goods

percentage Ⓐ (n) an amount of something, expressed as a number out of 100

savings (n) money that you put away, usually in a bank, for a later date

standard of living (n) how much money and comfort someone has

UNIT 1

▶ Great Egret and Dolphin Fishing Teamwork

The marshes of South Carolina are the location of an interesting fish tale.

There, these dolphins and egrets work together in a very special way.

These egrets are experts on the dolphins' behavior.

The moment a dolphin comes to the surface of the water and checks the nearest mud bank, the birds get ready for action.

Then, it happens. The dolphins push the fish onto the shore.

When the fish are out of the water, the dolphins start eating. But the egrets also join them for dinner.

This is the only place in the world where you can see this kind of behavior.

Strangely, the dolphins always use their right sides to push the fish to the shore.

The young dolphins learn this fishing technique from their parents, and so do the young egrets. Many of the birds now depend on the dolphins for their food. They never even fish for themselves. These egrets and dolphins demonstrate the ability of different animal species to work together in order to survive.

UNIT 2

▶ Colorado River, Grand Canyon, Yosemite

Some of the world's most beautiful natural environments are in the southwestern United States.

In just a few million years, the Colorado River has cut through parts of Arizona to form the Grand Canyon.

The Grand Canyon is 277 miles long and, in some places, 18 miles wide. At its deepest places, the river is a mile below the top of the canyon. It shows the effects of water and weather on the Earth's surface.

Its oldest rocks are almost 2 billion years old, nearly half the age of the Earth. This is the world's largest canyon, and the weather here can change dramatically. In the same day you can have hot, dry weather, followed by wind and snow. And every year the Colorado River cuts a little deeper into the bottom of the Grand Canyon.

Water also formed Carlsbad Caverns in New Mexico. Carlsbad is the largest, deepest cave system in North America. Even today water continues to change the inside of the caves. The results are spectacular.

Finally, high in the Sierra Mountains of California is Yosemite National Park. Its famous landmark Half Dome was made by the frozen water in a glacier moving through the canyon. Today the glaciers are gone, but water from the melting mountain snow flows throughout the national park.

Yosemite Falls drops nearly 2,500 feet—it's the tallest waterfall in North America.

UNIT 3

▶ The Jumbo Jet

Narrator: In 1969, a true giant of the skies first took flight. It could cross the Atlantic with enough fuel and twice as many passengers as any airplane before it. Now, there are nearly 1,000 of them. Each one is able to fly over 14 hours to their destinations without stopping. It's the 747—the jumbo jet—and this is the very first one.

Jimmy Barber helped build this very plane.

Jimmy Barber: Eight months straight you worked on the airplane, and we didn't just work, err, eight hours a day. Sometimes we worked 12 or more hours a day. And if it was necessary to sleep in your car in a parking lot, that's what you did. It was a highlight in my whole life was this aircraft, you know. Yeah. Wow, this is great.

Narrator: This is the first time Jimmy has been aboard since he worked on it over 45 years ago.

Jimmy Barber: This is great.

Narrator: When it first flew, this was the most modern plane in the air. It was the first double-decker jet in history with a fancy first-class lounge upstairs.

Jimmy Barber: And the upper deck, one airline turned that into a disco and put a dance floor up there. Another airline put piano bars in his … in these airplanes.

Narrator: But it was the enormous space downstairs that changed commercial air travel forever. With room for around 500 people, it started the age of low-cost air travel.

Since its first flight, engineers have redesigned the 747 fifteen times. Today it flies further and faster than ever before.

UNIT 4

▶ Halloween by the Numbers

Now, a little Halloween by the numbers. Tens of millions of trick-or-treaters are expected to hit the streets tomorrow. We purchase an estimated 600 million pounds of candy for Halloween, and if you haven't gotten to it yet, we are told that the most popular variety is— no surprise—chocolate. Other top costume choices include witches, pirates, and Batman. More than a billion pounds of pumpkins were grown last year. Illinois is the nation's number one pumpkin producing state. As for the origin of trick-or-treating, it is thought to have evolved from a Celtic tradition of putting out treats to placate the spirits who roam the streets during a sacred festival that marked the end of the Celtic year. Finally, you may be surprised to learn that there is nothing frightening about Halloween if you are a retailer. It is the second highest grossing holiday after Christmas. The National Retail Federation estimates the average person will spend nearly $75 on decorations, costumes and, of course, candy.

UNIT 5

▶ Nutrition Labels

Reporter: Today the Food and Drug Administration proposed a food label makeover. Jeff Pegues tells us it includes a reality check that some feel is long overdue.

Jeff Pegues: What and how people eat have changed. Now, for the first time in two decades, the labels on foods will change, too. The calories will be featured more prominently, and any added sugars or sweeteners will be listed as well. FDA commissioner Margaret Hamburg.

Margaret Hamburg: We're also asking for a change in serving size to reflect the realities of what people are eating.

Jeff Pegues: Here's what that means. The label on this pint of Ben & Jerry's chocolate chip cookie dough ice cream says each half-cup serving has 280 calories and 25% of the fat we should eat every day. Under the FDA proposal, the serving size would be a more realistic cup, which means each serving would contain 560 calories and 50% fat. At least publically, the food and beverage industry has been supportive. The Grocery Manufacturers Association says it's critical that any changes ultimately serve to inform and not confuse consumers. Some beverage companies, like PepsiCo, have already made changes, but what may be difficult for the industry to swallow, the overall price tag. A senior Obama administration official says the cost of implementing the changes could reach 2 billion dollars. First Lady Michelle Obama is a driving force behind the new labels.

Michelle Obama: As consumers and as parents, we have a right to understand what's in the food we're feeding our families, because that's really the only way that we can make informed choices.

Reporter: This is just a proposal, so there will be a public comment period. Nora, the FDA says it may be two years before consumers see these new labels on food in stores.

UNIT 6

▶ China's Man-made River

History is filled with stories of humans overcoming obstacles through discovery and invention. Take an enormous country like China. What do you do when most of your people live in the north, in cities like Beijing, but most of your water is in the south? You build an artificial river to bring water from the south to the north.

This river will be about 750 miles long when it is finished in 2030.

And this is it. A giant raised canal, or aqueduct—one of the largest engineering projects in the world.

Chinese workers and engineers are building the river piece by piece, in separate sections. Each section starts as a metal framework.

A team of 20 people build the metal frame. Then the concrete is added.

Finally, the section is moved into place using one of the world's most powerful cranes.

Each section weighs 1,200 tons—more than three commercial airplanes.

This woman operates the crane. It's a very important job, and it takes great skill.

She must work very carefully so that each section of the artificial river is in the perfect position.

The water will flow north to Beijing without using any pumps.

So the end of each section must be exactly 1 centimeter lower than the other end.

When the river is finished and operating in 2030, the water from the south will reach millions of Chinese people in the north.

UNIT 7

▶ A Life Tailored Around Clothes

Edgar Pomeroy: I'm Edgar Pomeroy. I grew up in Savannah, Georgia, and I knew I wanted to be a fashion designer when I was ten years old. Well, every day I used to watch my father get dressed because I would be watching cartoons or something on TV in their bedroom. And he was always putting on pinstripe suits and polka-dot ties and waistcoats and dressed to the nines, as they say. He was the only one I've ever known to mow the lawn in a Brooks Brothers button-down and khaki pants, and Weejuns, might I add. That's really how it all began.

Father: But you've always been able to put fabrics and colors together.

Edgar Pomeroy: Yeah, but look who I'm talking to. We're bespoke tailors as well as I'm more of a designer so we make our shirts and suits and all our clothes right here. We don't source anything out.

This is for a client that I'm seeing tomorrow. All the stripes match. The plaids come down. This is detail.

I'm upstairs when I'm in town pretty much all the time, checking the jackets and pants and seeing who's doing what. It has to fit. You can do the most beautiful cloth in the world but if you botch the cutting, it's over. It's just another piece of cloth that should be burned up in the floor. It got very lackadaisical in the 90s when the dot-com era came into play. And I was kind of disappointed because people kind of started dressing way down.

Some even looked like they just mowed their lawn. I dress people who love clothes. People who want to stand out, elegantly, of course. But they're dandies.

I didn't want to overkill this because you're conservative.

I go to their houses in Chicago, I go to L.A., I go to Baltimore, New York, London. I go all over. You know, I build a trust with them and I design for them. What I do is get to know their personality. If I go to their office or home, I look around, I see how it's decorated, I look at pictures, and I design around their personality. But I want them to take a little bit of a step out of their comfort zone. A little one, just to try. I let the client have the stage. I just kind of help them get to the stage.

UNIT 8

▶ Stock Market Crash of 1929

Narrator: On October 29, 1929, the New York Stock Exchange had its worst day ever— Black Tuesday. The stock market crashed, and investors lost billions of dollars in a single day. That day was the end of a decade of a strong U.S economy. It was the beginning of the Great Depression, the worst economic period in modern world history. During the next two years, stock prices fell 90%, banks and companies failed, and millions of people around the world lost their jobs.

Today you can visit the Museum of Financial History on Wall Street, in New York City, to learn more about what happened.

Man: So what we have here is the physical tape from October 29th, that Black Tuesday, and it's quite an important piece, it tells a great story.

Narrator: This is a replica of the machine that produced that ticker tape. The name *ticker tape* comes from the sound of the machine as it printed out the price of stocks and shares. But since the early 1970s, computers and electronic boards have reported the ups and downs in the stock market.

CREDITS

Text credits

Text on p. 32 adapted from 'Know the difference'. Copyright © Get Bear Smart Society. Reproduced with kind permission; Text on p. 166 adapted from 'Research Using the Internet' by W. Brock MacDonald and June Steel, University of Toronto. Reproduced with kind permission.

Photo credits

Key: T = Top, C = Center, B = Below, L = Left, R = Right, TL = Top Left, TC = Top Center, TR = Top Right, BL = Below Left, BR = Below Right, BG = Background.

p. 12: Cultura RM Exclusive/Peter Muller/Getty Images; pp. 14–15: Dangdumrong/Shutterstock; p. 19: Mark Newman/Lonely Planet Images/Getty Images; p. 23 (L): Ben Queenborough/Oxford Scientific/Getty Images; p. 23 (R): Marco Pozzi Photographer/Moment/Getty Images; p. 25: Miha Pavlin/Moment Select/Getty Images; p. 31: Jane Burton/Nature Picture Library/Getty Images; pp. 36–37: Paul Souders/Corbis Documentary/Getty Images; p. 41: Maximilian Müller/Moment/Getty Images; p. 45: Minden Pictures/Getty Images; pp. 58–59: Keren Su/China Span/Alamy; p. 62 (L): AFP/Getty Images; p. 62 (R): Bloomberg/Getty Images; p. 64: Karim Sahib/AFP/Getty Images; p. 67 (TL): Don Emmert/AFP/Getty Images; p. 67 (TC): pastorscott/E+/Getty Images; p. 67 (TR, BG): Gavin Hellier/robertharding/Getty Images; p. 70: Zoran Milich/Photonica/Getty Images; pp. 80–81: Jose Fuste Raga/Corbis Documentary/Getty Images; p. 86: ImagesBazaar/Getty Images; p. 89 (L): John Phillips/UK Press/Getty Images; p. 89 (C): Lumi Images/Dario Secen/Getty Images; p. 89 (R): Tommaso Boddi/WireImage/Getty Images; p. 91: Waseem Gashroo/Hindustan Times/Getty Images; p. 92: Sollina Images/Blend Images/Getty Images; pp. 102–103: Raphael Christinat/Shutterstock; p. 106 (photo a): Michael Heffernan/Taxi/Getty Images; p. 106 (photo b): Image Source/Getty Images; p. 106 (photo c): Kathrin Ziegler/Taxi/Getty Images; p. 106 (photo d): Resolution Productions/Blend Images/Getty Images; p. 106 (photo e): Ariel Skelley/Brand X Pictures/Getty Images; p. 106 (photo f): ViktorCap/iStock/Getty Images; p. 106 (photo g): Westend61/Getty Images; p. 106 (photo h): Tom M Johnson/Blend Images/Getty Images; p. 113: Ariel Skelley/Blend Images/Getty Images; pp. 124–125: STR/AFP/Getty Images; p. 129 (BG): hooky13/iStock/Getty Images; p. 129 (BL): Clouds Hill Imaging Ltd./Corbis Documentary/Getty Images; p. 129 (BR): Alex Wong/Getty Images News/Getty Images; p. 133 (photo 1): Victor Habbick/Visuals Unlimited/Getty Images; p. 133 (photo 2): Koichi Kamoshida/Getty Images News/Getty Images; p. 133 (photo 3): Izabela Habur/E+/Getty Images; pp. 146–147: Chelsea Lauren/Getty Images Entertainment/Getty Images; p. 151 (BR): Timothy Hiatt/Getty Images Entertainment/Getty Images; p. 151 (Carmen): mangostock/iStock/Getty Images; p. 151 (Ahmet): Jetta Productions/Blend Images/Getty Images; p. 152 (Jasmine): Atsushi Yamada/The Image Bank/Getty Images; p. 152 (Ben): Goodluz/iStock/Getty Images; p. 152 (Sara): Jacob Wackerhausen/iStock/Getty Images; p. 152 (Fatima), p. 188 (Zeyneb): Eugenio Marongiu/Cultura/Getty Images; p. 158: Alexander Spatari/Moment/Getty Images; pp. 168–169: Don Mason/Corbis/Getty Images; p. 173 (T): yodiyim/iStock/Getty Images; p. 173 (B): Heritage Images/Hulton Archive/Getty Images; p. 188 (Ahmed): Buero Monaco/Taxi/Getty Images; p. 188 (Margaux): Tim Robberts/Taxi/Getty Images; p. 188 (Li Wei): Shannon Fagan/Taxi/Getty Images.

Front cover photographs by (woman) Amazingmikael/Shutterstock and (BG) romakoma/Shutterstock.

Illustrations

by Oxford Designers & Illustrators p. 27; Simon Tegg p. 72.

Video Supplied by BBC Worldwide Learning.

Video Stills Supplied by BBC Worldwide Learning.

Corpus

Development of this publication has made use of the Cambridge English Corpus (CEC). The CEC is a multi-billion word computer database of contemporary spoken and written English. It includes British English, American English, and other varieties of English. It also includes the Cambridge Learner Corpus, developed in collaboration with the University of Cambridge ESOL Examinations. Cambridge University Press has built up the CEC to provide evidence about language use that helps to produce better language teaching materials

Cambridge Dictionaries

Cambridge dictionaries are the world's most widely used dictionaries for learners of English. The dictionaries are available in print and online at dictionary.cambridge.org. Copyright © Cambridge University Press, reproduced with permission.

Typeset by emc design ltd.

Classroom teachers shaped everything about *Prism*. The topics. The exercises. The critical thinking skills. The On Campus sections. Everything. We are confident that *Prism* will help your students succeed in college because teachers just like you helped guide the creation of this series.

Prism Advisory Panel

The members of the *Prism* Advisory Panel provided inspiration, ideas, and feedback on many aspects of the series. *Prism* is stronger because of their contributions.

Gloria Munson
University of Texas, Arlington

Dinorah Sapp
University of Mississippi

Kim Oliver
Austin Community College

Christine Hagan
George Brown College/Seneca College

Gregory Wayne
Portland State University

Heidi Lieb
Bergen Community College

Julaine Rosner
Mission College

Stephanie Kasuboski
Cuyahoga Community College

Global Input

Teachers from more than 500 institutions all over the world provided valuable input through:
- Surveys
- Focus Groups
- Reviews